The FRIENDSHIP BOOK

of Francis Gay

D. C. THOMSON & CO., LTD.
London Glasgow Manchester Dundee

A Thought
For Each Day
in 1999

There is no treasure the which may be
compared to a faithful friend.

Old English Ballad.

SHADY RILL

January

FRIDAY—JANUARY 1.

HERE'S a worthy recipe for us all at the start of another year:

NEW YEAR'S CAKE

1999 Doubts and Fears,
12 Months of Hurts,
7 Days of Tears,
6 Cups of Patience,
5 Cups of Peace,
4 Cups of Love,
3 Cups of Joy,
2 Helping Hands,
1 Large Heart.

Put the doubts, fears and hurts into a large saucepan. Pour in the tears and simmer until evaporated. Add 6 cups of patience, 4 of love, 3 of joy and 1 large heart.

Knead with 2 helping hands. Put on to a baking sheet and sprinkle with peace. Cook with tender care, allow to cool then cut into 365 small pieces.

Wrap in gold foil and freeze. Serve each day to the needy.

SATURDAY—JANUARY 2.

THERE are two important things to give your children — roots and wings.

THE FRIENDSHIP BOOK

SUNDAY—JANUARY 3.

INTO thine hand I commit my spirit: thou hast redeemed me, O Lord God of truth.

Psalms 31:5

MONDAY—JANUARY 4.

HAVE you made up your mind to change your ways and the direction of your life this New Year?

You have? Then perhaps you'll find helpful these words of Henry van Dyke, the American Presbyterian minister, poet, and essayist:

"Life is an arrow — therefore you must know what mark to aim at, how to use the bow."

TUESDAY—JANUARY 5.

A PRAYER

AS I go walking through the world,
Lord, walk along with me,
And through the beauty of the world,
Lord, help me look and see.
As I go listening through the world,
Lord, let me hear Your voice,
And with the wind, the birds, the sea,
Lord, help me to rejoice.
As I go slower through the world,
Lord, give me quiet peace,
And show me, always, in my life,
Your love will never cease.

Iris Hesselden.

WEDNESDAY—JANUARY 6.

VISITING that delightful town of Tewkesbury one day, I caught sight of this Wayside Pulpit:

"Life is a patchwork, and today we may begin a new design."

What stirring words to greet us on any day but maybe in particular, during the first month of a new year. To realise that we can create a fresh approach to how we go about things every day; can train our minds on kindly thoughts, so that when we look back on our quilt of life, we — and others — witnessed the beginning of a new bright patch.

THURSDAY—JANUARY 7.

I ONCE read that the heaviest cross you are called upon to bear is the one you see a loved one carrying for you. I remembered these words when I saw Winnie, a lady who had been caring for her invalid mother for years.

One day when I visited them, the old lady said to me, "I don't mind the pain or the inactivity so much, but my greatest trial is knowing that I have held back Winnie's life."

Personally, I thought it was just the reverse. Winnie, from being a rather thoughtless teenager, had grown into a caring and loving young woman who not only looked after her mother but was also a great asset in the village. I'm sure that she didn't think for a moment she was sacrificing her life for her mother.

THE FRIENDSHIP BOOK

FRIDAY—JANUARY 8.

A S I walked down the garden one bitterly cold day in January I noticed that the snowdrops and crocuses which had poked through the earth so bravely during the mild days of December had found the icy winds too much to bear and had stopped growing. Of course, when the sun shines and temperatures begin to rise, they will start to grow again and fulfil their early promise.

How like life, I thought. All too often a thoughtless word can send a sensitive person right back into their shell and it may require a great deal of patience to restore their confidence. It's so much better if we can avoid it happening in the first place.

SATURDAY—JANUARY 9.

A N elderly couple were celebrating their Golden Wedding. Their family arranged a party, and appropriately they received several gifts made of gold. Their grandchildren also wanted to contribute, but realised that anything made of gold was more than they could possibly afford. Then they had a bright idea.

Imagine their grandparents' delight and surprise when they were presented with a large box containing a whole host of golden goodies — a bag of golden delicious apples, golden-coloured marmalade, a tin of golden syrup and several other golden groceries.

Truly golden surprises!

THE FRIENDSHIP BOOK

SUNDAY—JANUARY 10.

TO every thing there is a season, and a time to every purpose under the heaven.

Ecclesiastes 3:1

MONDAY—JANUARY 11.

HAVE you ever noticed how older people and the very young can share so many things? They seem able to discover excitement together which the rest of us tend to miss.

If you hear a small voice exclaiming, "Come and look at this!" it might be a good idea to do just that. Who knows what you might find or where the path may lead?

It could be that little piece of the rainbow you lost, so many years ago.

TUESDAY—JANUARY 12.

WHEN the 19th-century American author Washington Irving lived in England he decided to go fishing one day. He was equipped with expensive tackle, yet he had no success.

Along came a small, rather shabby little boy. His rod was merely a long twig, a piece of string and a "vile earth worm"! In half an hour he had caught more fish than Irving had done in hours.

The best equipment does not always produce the best results if "know-how" is missing. The youngster had used what he possessed well. Now, this surely applies to life and our talents and possessions, too, doesn't it?

WEDNESDAY—JANUARY 13.

MY friend Hector likes to paint beautiful watercolours as a hobby. His pictures adorn not only the walls of his own house, but those of his family and friends, and he has donated many other paintings to raise funds for charity. I asked him once how he had first discovered his talent.

"Strangely enough, it was through what seemed, at the time, like very bad luck," he said. "You see, as a young man, I loved photography. One bright and sunny day I decided to cycle several miles to a local beauty spot but when I arrived, I was extremely upset to find that somewhere along the way, my camera had been lost.

"I'd come a long way, and the view was wonderful, so to make the best of things, I decided I'd draw some sketches in my notebook. It was so rewarding that I decided next time I went out for the day, I'd take a box of paints. I never did bother saving up for a new camera!"

It's not often you lose a camera and find a hidden talent instead.

THURSDAY—JANUARY 14.

IT can be a bit of a struggle getting out of bed on cold dark mornings, but our friend Rosie has the answer. She told me, "When I wake up I ask myself, 'What can I look forward to today?' There's always something, you know, even if it's quite small. After that I just jump out of bed."

Try it!

FRIDAY—JANUARY 15.

ON 6th June, 1844 George Williams and a group of his young friends met in a little room over a draper's shop in St Paul's Churchyard, London.

They were very concerned about the welfare of others like themselves — shop assistants living away from home without any Christian influence. They prayed and planned, and from that meeting The Young Men's Christian Association was born.

Little did George Williams and his friends with their unselfish work and great determination realise what they were creating for other young men in the future, throughout the world.

Everything worthwhile starts with a single step.

SATURDAY—JANUARY 16.

SOME neighbours of ours who live next door to each other were never particularly friendly. Then, in the middle of one Winter's night, a pipe burst at Stan's home. His first thought was of Jim next door, who was a plumber. Being an expert at the job, Jim was soon able to complete the necessary repair.

When Summer came round again, it gave Stan — an excellent gardener — the opportunity to repay Jim for his help by giving him lots of home-grown produce. All because of a burst pipe they now get on well, and have struck up a friendship after years of indifference.

By sharing our skills with others, we can add happiness and a real meaning to life.

SUNDAY—JANUARY 17.

IN the beginning God created the heaven and the earth.

Genesis 1:1

MONDAY—JANUARY 18.

ZANE GREY is remembered as a prolific writer of Western novels, many of which are still as popular as when he first wrote them. The other day I came across his recipe for greatness:

To bear up under loss;
To fight the bitterness of defeat and
the weakness of grief;
To be victor over anger;
To smile when tears are close;
To resist disease and evil men and base instincts;
To hate hate and to love love;
To go on when it would seem good to die;
To look up with unquenchable faith
in something ever more about to be.

That is what any man can do, and be great.

TUESDAY—JANUARY 19.

DO you have a favourite quote from a bookmark? This one's from my collection: "Thank you for loving me, even when I am unlovable."

It makes you pause and think how you're not always the person you would like to be. It reminds you also, how fortunate you are that Somebody loves you, in spite of your many faults.

WEDNESDAY—JANUARY 20.

ONCE we had a holiday home in a remote spot, lit by candles and oil lamps, which meant, of course, no television, no radio, not even an easily-made cup of tea. We sat in flickering candlelight, wondering what to talk about.

Then the Lady of the House said, "Do you remember that evening at dusk when we saw the deer come down to drink?" Indeed I did — we knew there were deer in the area, but had never seen one, until a farmer told us where to watch at dusk. It was a magical moment.

Then we continued our reminiscing. "Do you remember . . . that canal holiday when you fell into the lock? . . . that morning we saw that young blue-tit family take their first flight?" On and on we went, recalling more and more delightful reminiscences.

What a blessing memory is. Yes, it can recall unhappy times, too, I know, but banish them from your mind. Instead, concentrate on the joys of yesteryear, letting them become candles shedding a golden light on the present and the path ahead.

THURSDAY—JANUARY 21.

BY WAY OF THANKS . . .

*T**HE simplest word can often seem*
  The hardest one to say,
But when it comes to gratitude
  A thank-you leads the way!

Elizabeth Gozney.

FRIDAY—JANUARY 22.

I HAVE a liking for antique fairs. You never know what you may come across, do you?

Once the Lady of the House and I discovered a vase, identical to one we had once owned. We had treasured ours for many years, but the day came when it met with an untimely end. By then, Dorothy, who gave it to us, had become a close friend. However, no sooner had we decided to buy this replacement, than someone stepped in before us and went off happily with their purchase.

We shrugged resignedly, then smiled at each other and hoped it would give the new owner much pleasure. On the way home, we remembered ruefully that Dorothy would be visiting us the following day.

"Don't you think, Francis," said the Lady of the House, "that friendship is much more important than possessions?"

A vase can be replaced but true friends are priceless.

SATURDAY—JANUARY 23.

BROTHER ABSOLM was a medieval English monk who was renowned for his honesty. Once he went to the Father and confessed that he had forgotten to say a certain prayer on a certain day.

"Why do you tell me this?" the Father asked. "If you hadn't, no one would ever have known."

"No, but I would have known," Absolm replied simply.

SUNDAY—JANUARY 24.

ARISE, shine; for thy light is come, and the glory of the Lord is risen upon thee.

Isaiah 60:1

MONDAY—JANUARY 25.

WHAT is success? John Buchan, the popular Scottish novelist who rose to become Lord Tweedsmuir, Governor-General of Canada, had no doubts on the matter.

"Success," he said, "is not making a lot of money or attaining a great position or fame. It is doing sound work in which you are happy, and becoming, in the doing of it, braver and wiser and kinder."

TUESDAY—JANUARY 26.

I'M not complaining,
  Just explaining
How things now are with me —
  Can't climb the stairs
Or rise from chairs,
  Without some help, you see.

I'm not complaining
  Just explaining,
My speeds now are "Dead Slow" and "Stop".
  My get up and go
Is painfully slow
  But don't worry — I'll come out on top!
            Dorothy M. Loughran.

WEDNESDAY—JANUARY 27.

SPEAKING one day to Lilian, who was staying near our home while on a short visit, I was taken back many decades.

Lilian, who is 90, clearly remembered seeing her mother drawing water from a well and carrying it to the kitchen for drinking and cooking purposes. On wash days, however, water had to be collected from the rainwater butts in the garden.

"It was very hard work," Lilian remembered, "as the containers were so heavy. It was just wonderful the day water could be obtained from a tap. Pure joy!"

Nowadays, we take for granted that water appears when we turn on the tap, don't we? It is indeed one of life's blessings always to be grateful for, so the next time you use water, remember Lilian's mother, and count your blessings.

THURSDAY—JANUARY 28.

"HAVE you seen my favourite television programme yet, Grandma?" asked young Nathan. He then went on to describe it enthusiastically, and Grandma pulled a face.

"No, I haven't," she replied, "and I'm sure I wouldn't like it!"

"Oh, Grandma," Nathan scolded, "you can't say that you don't like something if you've never tried it."

Oh, dear, thought Grandma, I wonder where I heard these words before?

FRIDAY—JANUARY 29.

STANDING on a river bank one day, I noticed that the water had been churned up and made very murky by a great swathe of water weed. But even as I watched, the current swiftly bore the weed away, leaving the water clear and sparkling again.

I couldn't help thinking how like life that was. One minute everything seems black and miserable, but things can change quite rapidly — so do not despair if things are not looking too good at the moment. Like the water weed, troubles will be carried away downstream and you will have a new perspective on life.

SATURDAY—JANUARY 30.

"I HAVE heard it said that everyone has four selves," a philosophy student once said to his tutor. "Myself as I really am. Myself as I think I am. Myself as others see me and myself as I think they see me. What do you think?"

"I think that you shouldn't analyse yourself too much," came the reply. "Just be yourself! Oh, and take Shakespeare's advice — to thine own self be true!"

SUNDAY—JANUARY 31.

AND they were all filled with the Holy Ghost, and began to speak with other tongues, as the Spirit gave them utterance.

Acts 2:4

February

A T church we were once told a story about a chapel in Wales which needed a new minister. A suitable young man was presented as a candidate and he met with the approval of all the congregation but one — a lady who expressed her misgivings forcibly.

When this young man began his ministry, the objector stayed away from Sunday services to show her disapproval. Deciding to do his best to put things right, the minister called to see her. He knocked on the door, but there was no reply. He knocked again — there was still no reply.

Feeling sure there was someone in, he stooped down to look through the keyhole. To his surprise his eye saw an eye on the other side of the door!

As time passed, both people concerned were able to laugh about the incident. "Well, we are able to see eye to eye about things now," said she.

"Yes," said the minister, "but we both had to get down on our knees first."

G ET on the right train of thought and you'll reach the right station. The wrong one can lead you off the rails.

WEDNESDAY—FEBRUARY 3.

HAVE you ever heard of the Fir Cone Movement?

It began a few years ago in Birmingham. So many people seemed to be retiring from their regular jobs at an earlier age that a group met to form a retirement council and initiated courses to prepare people for a more positive attitude to retirement. So many benefited from this that they formed Friends In Retirement — F.I.R.

Their symbol is the fir cone of the larch tree, a tree which bends but does not easily break. The cone which bears the seeds of new life usually remains on the tree throughout Autumn and Winter. The larch's main growing season takes place in Springtime, but a secondary growth occurs near the base of many cones in Autumn.

Older folk have plenty to offer, and the Fir Cone Movement is living proof of this, encouraging all who participate in it.

THURSDAY—FEBRUARY 4.

I CAME across this quotation from John Ruskin and I'd like to share it with you today:

"Let every dawn of morning be to you as the beginning of life and every setting sun be to you as its close. Let every one of these short lives leave behind its record of something done for others and for God."

It's something to think about as we embark on the precious gift of another new day.

LOOKING AND
LEARNING

FRIDAY—FEBRUARY 5.

IT is February, perhaps one of the least favourite of months when days are short and cold, nights are long and we can expect snow and ice.

Yet there are so many things that can give us pleasure in February — the absolute stillness and beauty of a fall of snow in the early morning before footsteps and car tracks have marred it; the comfort of a steaming bowl of porridge for breakfast; the antics of blue tits hanging from a string of nuts in the garden — all viewed from the warmth of our living-room window. Then, in a sunny corner of the garden amid the melting snow, the first snowdrop reminds us that Spring will soon be on the way.

Yes, there is surely a lot to lift our spirits!

SATURDAY—FEBRUARY 6.

I HAVE been reading an article explaining how some people do not take opportunities in life when they are presented to them. I remember my grandfather saying, "If you will not when you may, you may not when you will."

It may be an old saying, but it is surely good advice, well worth keeping in mind today.

SUNDAY—FEBRUARY 7.

PRAISE ye the Lord for it is good to sing praises unto our God; for it is pleasant; and praise is comely.

Psalms 147:1

MONDAY—FEBRUARY 8.

I WONDER if, like me, you enjoy the stories of Captain Horatio Hornblower by C. S. Forester? The inspiration to write a book about historical naval adventures came to him when he bought some books on the Napoleonic Wars in a dusty second-hand bookshop in Harwich.

C. S. Forester was born in Cairo in 1899, and from boyhood was always interested in model ships. He was sent to Dulwich College where he never really shone at anything. He then studied medicine at Guy's Hospital but left without a degree. After these disappointments he turned to writing — at last with success. He went on to write 30 or more novels which have sold in huge numbers.

He worked exceptionally hard all his life. He is no longer with us, but we do have his famous fictional hero who was born in his author's fertile imagination in that dusty second-hand bookshop by the sea. With C.S. Forester's imagination and dedication, no wonder Captain Hornblower is still so much admired today.

TUESDAY—FEBRUARY 9.

OUR friend Jim has had a few ups and downs in his time but he takes them all philosophically. "I've always found," he said to me recently, "that when life knocks you flat on your back, it certainly puts you in a grand position for looking up!"

THE FRIENDSHIP BOOK

A FRIEND is someone, who will lend
An ear, if one's required,
Or at another time extend
A hand if so desired.

A friend is someone, who can be
A rock in times of stress;
Steadfast should adversity
Endanger happiness.

A friend is someone, who can win
Your trust in times of strife,
And prove a priceless asset in
The highs and lows of life.

J. M. Robertson.

"SMILE, please!" That's what photographers sometimes say, and it is what we should try to do in everyday life, too.

I once met a glum-looking young mother pushing a small girl in a buggy. She was a lovely child and I smiled at her. Her beam in my direction was wonderful to receive in return. What's more, her mother managed to raise a smile, too, and then I could clearly see where the little girl had got her good looks!

It is sad that we have to have a "Smile Day" to remind us of the pleasure this can give to others and also light up our own lives at the same time.

FRIDAY—FEBRUARY 12.

I ONCE read this German saying and I'd like to share it with you today:

"A good neighbour doubles the value of a house".

How true this is!

SATURDAY—FEBRUARY 13.

WHENEVER St Valentine's Day comes around, I think of my young friend, Patricia, who works as a care assistant and occupational therapist in a home for the elderly.

One year she decided that she couldn't allow 14th February to pass without doing something special, so she organised an afternoon "Valentine Tea Dance". The room was decorated with hearts and flowers, and favourite "Old Time" dance tunes were played. Tea was served at individual tables set with embroidered cloths and tiny vases of flowers, and there were dainty sandwiches, heart-shaped biscuits and a beautiful iced cake.

It was a lovely way to brighten a February afternoon, and the guests declared it the best day for a long time. If some of them encouraged the romantic atmosphere by exchanging Valentine cards — how appropriate!

SUNDAY—FEBRUARY 14.

IN every thing give thanks: for this is the will of God in Christ Jesus concerning you.

Thessalonians I 5:18

MONDAY—FEBRUARY 15.

GROUP Captain Sir Douglas Bader, when a young pilot in the R.A.F., lost both his legs in a flying accident. For many that would have been the end of flying, but not for Bader. He mastered the use of artificial legs, and in 1939 on the outbreak of war he returned to the R.A.F. to win for himself a place in flying history.

I feel sure Douglas Bader would have agreed with the following lines from "Bishop Blougram's Apology" written by Robert Browning, the Victorian poet:

The common problem, yours, mine, everyone's,
Is — not to fancy what were fair in life
Provided it could be — but, finding first
What may be, then find how to make it fair
Up to our means.

Perhaps you will find these lines helpful, when you have a dark and difficult time in your life, and things are far from easy.

TUESDAY—FEBRUARY 16.

THERE are ways of complaining which are more tactful than others. Take this example:

"Oh, Mr Noakes," began a customer, smiling at the shopkeeper in her local shop, "do you remember the dozen eggs I bought last week?"

"Yes, madam."

"Well, I thought I'd let you know that ten of them were fresh."

Mr Noakes nodded and smiled. "It will be my pleasure to replace the other two, madam."

WEDNESDAY—FEBRUARY 17.

DO you have a favourite hymn that means a lot to you? Our friend, Connie, was telling us about the one that is special to her family, going back to the time of her grandmother. Rather than use the first line of the hymn each time, her family knew it by its number, 494, in the book "Sacred Songs And Hymns" by Moody and Sankey.

Connie told us that when her son was reported missing in the Falklands War, he had eventually managed to send her a telegram. He ended his brief message with "494".

Apparently, he had been asked about the significance of this number and had explained that it was the family hymn, always put on letters and said when parting.

You must now be wondering what the words of that hymn are. The first line is:

"God be with you 'til we meet again."

THURSDAY—FEBRUARY 18.

HERE are two pieces of encouragement from two different members of the famous American family, the Roosevelts.

Theodore, who was a popular President, said that the road to success was "to do what you can, with what you have, where you are."

Eleanor, the well-loved wife of Franklin D. Roosevelt, who was also a President, wrote: "What one has to do usually can be done."

FRIDAY—FEBRUARY 19.

SOMETIMES after visiting a particularly attractive town or area, either for a long holiday or merely a day trip, you can find yourself wishing you lived there all the time. A slight sense of discontent with your present surroundings might start to niggle.

I was feeling a bit like this during one stay away from home when I noticed these words of advice outside St John's Church in Bolling, Bradford:

"It doesn't matter where you live,
As long as you live where you are."

Just then that advice seemed to be meant for me!

SATURDAY—FEBRUARY 20.

EDWARD, a successful businessman, says that the best lesson he ever had was when he was a boy and his father told him to build a tower of dominoes. He did so.

"Now," said his father, "knock it down." It immediately fell in a heap.

"You see," observed his father, "how much better it looked when it was standing? Always be a builder, not a knocker-down!"

Good advice for everyone, surely.

SUNDAY—FEBRUARY 21.

HE shall feed his flock like a shepherd: he shall gather the lambs with his arm and carry them in his bosom.

Isaiah 40:11

MONDAY—FEBRUARY 22.

THE Lady of the House and our friend Mary are patchwork enthusiasts, and along with some other friends were busy sewing a patchwork quilt for charity.

"I think, Francis," the Lady of the House said to me, "our quilt would make a lovely and original wedding present, as we have chosen the old American 'Wedding Ring' pattern, which symbolises the joining of two lives in peace and harmony. But our Quilting Bee also calls it our 'Friendship Quilt', and so it is, for while we sew we are enjoying friendly companionship and working together.

Friendship, companionship, peace and harmony — surely a precious small bouquet of the good things of life.

TUESDAY—FEBRUARY 23.

A DELEGATE to an international Christian youth conference was trying to sell cassettes of gospel singing. He approached a smiling African. "Would you like to buy one?" he asked.

"But I have no player!"

"You could borrow one."

"I have no electricity!"

"You could keep it in your home until you do."

"But I have no home!"

Said the delegate afterwards, "I have forgotten all the speeches made that week, but that smiling African — I'll never forget him."

MORNING HAS BROKEN

WEDNESDAY—FEBRUARY 24.

THE streams of life are swiftly flowing
Through the sunshine and the shade,
Bearing many hopes and wishes
And the promises we made.
Through the joyful Summer meadows,
Over pebble, rock and stone,
Sometimes quiet and unheeded
As we travel on alone.
Surging through the storms of Winter,
Sparkling as the Spring appears,
Reflecting all our love and laughter,
Cherished through so many years.
The streams of life, forever flowing,
Showing time is but a span,
Treasure every fleeting moment,
Catch the sunshine while you can.

Iris Hesselden.

THURSDAY—FEBRUARY 25.

THERE are many old sundial inscriptions to be found. Our garden sundial just says briefly: "Count only the sunny hours."

Not so the motto composed "For Katrina's Sundial" by Dr Henry Van Dyke, the American statesman and poet:

"Hours fly, flowers die,
New days, new ways
Pass by, love stays."

These lines express a timeless truth, I think you'll agree!

FRIDAY—FEBRUARY 26.

WE visited our friends Alec and Jane one day; Jane had been very ill. As we walked round the neat garden, Jane looked across to the one next door. There were two trees — one in a sorry state, the other, a healthy specimen.

"I feel just like that old tree today," remarked Jane. Before I could reply, Alec said, "You're not a bit like that, love. To me you're like that beautiful young tree beside it."

Jane's smile proved that Alec had said just the right words to uplift her. Truly, a few words of encouragement can work wonders.

SATURDAY—FEBRUARY 27.

SIR WILL Y. DARLING was a popular Lord Provost of Edinburgh in the 1940s. He was also a successful author. As a young man he had gone to work in London, and his mother asked him to be sure to remember to write.

"I did," he later recalled. "I wrote every week for years." He was more proud of those letters than of all his other writings.

SUNDAY—FEBRUARY 28.

LET your light so shine before men, that they may see your good works and glorify your Father which is in heaven.

Matthew 5:16

March

MONDAY—MARCH 1.

HOW can you tell when Spring has arrived? The first swallow? An early primrose? The call of the cuckoo? I rather like the 18th-century country saying: "When you can tread on nine daisies at once, Spring has come."

Try it!

TUESDAY—MARCH 2.

NOWADAYS we probably think of Japan as a focus of the electronic industry. I was reminded when I was reading a book one evening, that the country is still part of the mystic East and its ancient philosophy, and I learned about an inscription panel in the gardens of an ancient temple in Kyoto.

It gives advice on how to reach a ripe old age. Be economical with salt, meat, sugar, food in general, trouble, anger, talk, car-riding and also material desires. On the other hand it does recommend generosity in vegetables, fruit, chewing, sleep, laughter, activity, bathing, walking and giving.

There is surely much to be said for this way of thinking; television sets and cars are not the only good things to come from Japan!

WEDNESDAY—MARCH 3.

A MAN once went into a bank and said, "I want to draw out a hundred pounds, please." The bank clerk checked the man's account, then replied, "I'm sorry, sir, but you cannot take out that amount because you haven't put anything into your account for so long — in fact, you are on the point of being overdrawn!"

An old, old story, yet ever new. If we fail to put anything into life, to make the most of what we've got — for ourselves, for others — then we won't get a lot out! It's as simple as that.

THURSDAY—MARCH 4.

WHEN the Lady of the House revisited her home town, she was invited to have tea with her schoolfriend Dorothy whom she hadn't seen for a number of years. Consequently there was much happy conversation about the old days — and the present — as they were brought up to date with news of former pupils.

Then Dorothy brought out her autograph album in which so many had left their mark — pages signed by teachers and school prefects, little pen and ink drawings or watercolour paintings by friends, as well as the usual sprinkling of humorous verse and "words of wisdom".

So that old autograph album brought back many happy memories that afternoon. It's always good to make new friends — but let's never forget the old ones!

FRIDAY—MARCH 5.

ONE of the most moving radio interviews I have ever heard was given by the actor Paul Eddington, shortly before his death. He was suffering from a form of skin cancer, but was facing the situation resolutely and calmly.

When asked how he would like people to think of him, he replied, "I would like them to say, 'He did very little harm', and you know, that's not very easy."

It may not be very easy but I'm sure in Paul Eddington's brave case it was certainly true, and on the way he did a great deal of good.

SATURDAY—MARCH 6.

ONE Spring morning I received a parcel from Switzerland. On the lid of the box inside was a beautiful picture of the little wild narcissi which grow in profusion on the Alpine slopes and fields in Springtime. The customs label read "Fleurs Naturelles Sans Valeur" (wild flowers without value).

The tiny flowers, in bud, soon recovered from their journey, opening out their delicate blooms and filling the air with an exquisite perfume. What immense pleasure they gave for many a day!

Sans valeur? — I don't think so.

SUNDAY—MARCH 7.

AND whatsoever you do, do it heartily, as to the Lord and not unto men.

Colossians 3:23

THE FRIENDSHIP BOOK

I WALKED along the road one day, gazing at a line of parked cars. So many had stickers on their windows and I became interested in the wording. My favourites were these:

"Life is fragile. Handle with prayer."

Then a cheerfully-painted face bore the words: "Smile, God loves you."

This last one sent me home, not only smiling, but with a song in my heart. I think we should all have this particular sticker in a place where we could see it every morning.

Now, what a happy start to the day that would make!

THE TWO OF US

SHE really thinks I'm wonderful,
Of that there's little doubt.
Something in her manner bears
This brave assumption out.

The moment that she takes my hand,
It makes me so aware
A certain kind of chemistry
Is obviously there.

It's true I'm so much older,
But in my heart I know
That when she calls me "Grandad" —
I'm her very special beau!

J. M. Robertson.

WEDNESDAY—MARCH 10.

THE story is told of a young Italian who was apprenticed to an artist specialising in mosaics. The apprentice noticed that his master often threw away little bits of stone and glass, and the young man began picking up the fragments his master had rejected. Some he threw away, others he kept, and then he began to make a picture.

Years later, his master discovered his former apprentice's work, and declared that it was the work of a skilled craftsman, though he had no idea of its origin. Then his one-time apprentice confessed that he himself had made that picture, little by little, out of the tiny rejected pieces of stone and glass.

Very little in life need go to waste — discarded pieces can so often be reassembled to make a worthwhile whole.

THURSDAY—MARCH 11.

I WAS amused to hear the tale of the physics teacher who asked his class, "Can anyone tell me what happens when a body is submerged in water?"

"Yes, sir," responded a bright pupil immediately, "the telephone rings!"

If friends sometimes ring our doorbell or phone us at rather inconvenient times, we really ought to chuckle. After all, it would be no laughing matter if friends never called.

FRIDAY—MARCH 12.

I DON'T make a habit of eavesdropping, but the woman in the queue ahead *was* speaking rather loudly!

"I used to get really discouraged," she was telling her friend, "about how little I seemed to accomplish each day. I even made long lists of jobs that needed doing, but every time I checked how many I hadn't managed, it got me down."

"So what changed?" asked her companion.

"I did!" laughed the woman. "Instead of always nagging myself about all the chores I had left undone, I realised I could write a list of all the things I had managed during the day. By the time I'd added everything together, such as calling on old Mrs Brown, fetching a prescription for the young mum next-door, and writing letters to friends, the list looked really impressive. It may sound strange, but now that I've stopped worrying, I seem to get more done."

Isn't it amazing how such a simple and positive change of viewpoint can work wonders?

SATURDAY—MARCH 13.

THIS is part of a lovely Hungarian blessing:

Where there is belief, there is love,
Where there is love, there is peace,
Where there is peace, there is grace,
Where there is grace, there is God.

SUNDAY—MARCH 14.

BUT the word of the Lord endureth for ever. And this is the word which by the gospel is preached unto you.

Peter 1 1:25

MONDAY—MARCH 15.

OVER the years, I've had a great deal of enjoyment from outdoor pursuits such as walking and rambling. Hillsides and mountain tops are, for many people, magnetic, and climbers and walkers are drawn back to them time and time again. Speaking to other outdoor enthusiasts, I have found that on a mountain people experience the same oneness between themselves and the sense of infinity which I do.

"I to the hills will lift mine eyes" — not only the psalmist, but many a soul in distress has gained inspiration from the peaks.

TUESDAY—MARCH 16.

THE man on the bus smiled. "I've been working in Tenerife for eighteen months and I've been looking forward to this," he remarked.

I suddenly saw the fields and trees as he must have been seeing them. Everything looked so fresh and green and even the rain was refreshing. I know many people enjoy a holiday in the sun, but aren't we fortunate to have such beautiful scenery and a changeable climate?

WEDNESDAY—MARCH 17.

SOME friends of ours have recently moved house, and against their front door is the name of their abode, "Thistledome".

There have never been any thistles in that area, so I was curious to know why they had chosen that particular name for their new home. I was told: "We'd been searching long enough for a suitable house, and when we found this one, I said, 'This'll do me', and my wife said: 'Me, too'. So there we are!"

Not so much "Thistledome", but "This'll do me".

THURSDAY—MARCH 18.

HAVE you heard the story of the professor at one of our universities who bought a small concertina in a junk shop? It was only a humble instrument but he learned to play it, giving much pleasure to himself and others.

One of his students was from a wealthy family. "Say," he said, "I would like to play like that. If I get an instrument, will you have the time to give me some lessons?"

The professor agreed and the next time they met, the student had the largest and most expensive-looking accordion you could imagine. Lessons began but progress was slow. At last in exasperation the student said, "I can't get the hang of this clumsy instrument. How about swapping mine for yours?"

I'm sure there's a lesson in this somewhere!

FARMYARD
FRIENDS

FRIDAY—MARCH 19.

WHAT can you do when you have a problem that simply refuses to go away? Just sitting worrying about it won't help.

Some years ago I was given some advice which I'd like to pass on. Take a piece of paper and write down the worst possible outcome of your present worries. Be completely honest with yourself — this is for your eyes alone.

Fold the paper very small, put it in the corner of a drawer, then leave it there for two weeks. Now, try to forget all about it and get on with life.

At the end of the fortnight, take it out, unfold it and read your thoughts. You will be quite surprised at what you had written, and I'm sure you'll find things turned out much better than you expected. All this will surely go to prove, once again, that worry alone never cures anything.

Hope, faith and trust can accomplish so much more.

SATURDAY—MARCH 20.

I CAME across H. C. Turnbull's words of appreciation for mothers recently:

"The highest wages in the world are earned by good mothers. The mother who does an honest day's work, week in and week out, in faithful care of her children, is on a large salary and she will be rich, sooner or later."

So to mothers everywhere on Mothering Sunday, God bless you all!

SUNDAY—MARCH 21.

D EPART from evil, and do good; seek peace, and pursue it.

Psalms 34:14

MONDAY—MARCH 22.

W HEN I called to see my friend George, who is a headmaster, he had just finished writing a reference for a member of his staff who was applying for a new post.

"It's something that always takes a lot of thought, Francis," he said, "because I try to write what will be most helpful. After all, a person's whole future may be in my hands and I wouldn't want to do anything to cloud his or her chances."

How true, I thought. In all our comings and goings we each have the opportunity to be either "a stumbling block or a stepping stone".

I feel sure we would all prefer to be the latter.

TUESDAY—MARCH 23.

T AKE time to think and look around you,
Smell the flowers, see the sky,
Let your hopeful thoughts surround you,
Never let your daydreams die.
Take time to listen, time for caring,
Counting blessings from above,
Time to know the joy of sharing,
And the precious gift of love.

Iris Hesselden.

THE FRIENDSHIP BOOK

FRED lives in a special home for elderly people. It is special because Betty is the matron there. She has known him for a long time — after all, he's her father!

She once told me something about this modest man. He is still always ready to help folk in any way he can, but is always unassuming in the way he gives his help.

"Once," she said, "a young boy was stranded on a lake. Onlookers did nothing, but Dad rescued him and took him home."

Fred's story of thoughtfulness and helpfulness went on. Betty says that one day he organised a game of football for some youngsters. He put a girl in a wheelchair to keep goal so that she wouldn't be left out — everyone had fun.

We give thanks for people like Fred and his acts of kindness, and will always remember the tribute paid to him by his daughter.

TOM loved growing vegetables so much that he filled his front garden with cabbages amongst the flowers.

One day his neighbour leaned over the gate and said, "You've got so many caterpillars on your cabbages, Tom, that I can almost hear them munching. You'll have to put salt on them."

"Nay, lad," replied Tom. "If they don't like them as they are, they can do without."

FRIDAY—MARCH 26.

A LITTLE boy and his mother were hurrying home one day. Then Sam noticed two large balloons — one yellow, one green — bobbing about at someone's front door. His mother explained that it must be a birthday party, as she could see lots of cards on the window-sill.

After a few minutes Sam asked, "Mummy, is that a happy house where those balloons are?" She replied that she was sure it was.

"Then why don't we have them on our door? Ours is a happy house, isn't it?"

If we all tried to take a more cheerful approach to life, the world would be a brighter place.

SATURDAY—MARCH 27.

I HAVE yet to meet someone who doesn't worry about the future. It's difficult sometimes not to do this, but I always remember that life comes in little bits — nights cut off each day, with tomorrow a new start.

Let's be thankful for each "cut-off" bit of life when we can renew our strength. A new day always dawns afresh for us to tackle life's problems and help others to solve theirs.

SUNDAY—MARCH 28.

T HOU shalt love the Lord thy God with all thine heart, and with all thy soul, and with all thy might.

Deuteronomy 6: 5

NET WORK

MONDAY—MARCH 29.

I ONCE happened to come across an old 16th-century proverb — "Kitchen physic is best physic" — in a book I'd borrowed.

I paused to think about it. Four hundred years had gone by since the adage had first been coined, and during that time vast strides in medical science have been made, yet I still felt convinced of the wisdom contained in these words. Much as I sincerely appreciate the skills of our scientists, surgeons, doctors and nurses, there is undoubtedly something special about the healing power of our own home that beats all other medicine.

As our gardening friend Elspeth put it: "I know the hospital did a wonderful job of re-staking my branches, but now I'm back on home ground, I can really spread my roots!"

TUESDAY—MARCH 30.

COME and see what I've got!" said old Bill excitedly. I followed him up the stairs to his tiny top flat. In the ceiling was a brand-new skylight and he beamed as I gazed up at the blue sky.

"I call it my window to Heaven," he said.

From now on every skylight will be to me a "window to Heaven".

WEDNESDAY—MARCH 31.

YOU can't see the bright side? Then polish up the dull one!

April

APRIL is here again and how glad we are to welcome this month. It is many people's favourite time, and from abroad, poet Robert Browning wrote, "Oh, to be in England now that April's there."

The name derives from the Latin word for "opening", and all around us we can see the countryside being re-clothed in its new Spring dress as buds and blossom appear again. The bowling season starts and we can begin to enjoy all our other outdoor activities once more. House martins, swifts and swallows will soon return and begin building nests under our eaves, while any day we will be able to say we have heard the first cuckoo. A sure sign of Spring!

Robert Burns expresses it beautifully:

> *Now blooms the lily on the bank,*
> *The primrose down the brae;*
> *The hawthorn's budding in the glen*
> *And milk-white is the slae.*

FRIDAY—APRIL 2.

DON'T wait for something to turn up. Get busy and turn it up yourself.

SATURDAY—APRIL 3.

IT was quite a small Easter card. Pretty and uplifting, but not expensive. The Lady of the House chose it for the words, and sent it to an elderly lady who lived alone.

We had almost forgotten about it, when a little note arrived. It had obviously been written with much effort, and in a wavering hand. Chrissie thanked us for the kind thought and finished by sending us her blessings at this special time.

How wonderful that someone in failing health could still consider others so much! And how lovely that our card seemed to give so much pleasure.

Isn't this what the spirit of Easter is all about?

SUNDAY—APRIL 4.

AND said unto them, Thus it is written, and thus it behoved Christ to suffer, and to rise from the dead the third day.

Luke 24:46

MONDAY—APRIL 5.

WILLIAM PENN, the well-known 17th-century Quaker, once described the nature of friendship thus:

"A true friend unbosoms freely; assists readily; adventures boldly; takes all patiently; defends courageously and continues a friend unchangeably."

Surely these are words to keep in mind today.

TUESDAY—APRIL 6.

WARM Easter wishes —
For hope and for peace,
For love and contentment
To grow and increase;
For joy in abundance
And dreams coming true,
For bright Easter gladness
All the year through.

Iris Hesselden.

WEDNESDAY—APRIL 7.

I WAS in a natural history museum when I suddenly noticed a group gathering round an illuminated box in a corner. I joined them and the crowd grew, as someone cried, "Look — that one moved!"

Everyone's attention was focused on an incubator. An egg shook — then a crack appeared in the shell. A tiny beak thrust through the space, next a wing. The crack widened further. The fragile chick, feathers sticking to its skin, took a few shuddering breaths and strained against the shell.

"Come on," urged a little girl, "you can do it!"

The shell eventually fell away and out flopped the new creature, to the cheers of its admiring audience.

We can get so carried away with modern technology that we can all too easily forget the beauty and wonder to be found around us in apparently ordinary situations.

THE FRIENDSHIP BOOK

<u>THURSDAY—APRIL 8.</u>

IT was a windy day, and as the Lady of the House and I left the supermarket a gust caught someone's handkerchief and it fluttered away down the road.

"Don't bother about it," said its owner as someone began to chase after it. "It's only an old one." And so he let it go. Someone nearby remarked that it is often the old possessions which we feel most comfortable with.

Well, there's a lot to be said for the "lift" and excitement that something new gives us. But for real satisfaction I'll settle for the things I'm most comfortable with — my old sweater, my old slippers — and, best of all, my old friends.

<u>FRIDAY—APRIL 9.</u>

WHO can resist a bargain? Well, here's one that's not just any old bargain — it's free and it's labelled Springtime! Even in the most built-up parts of cities with drab streets everywhere, there will be signs of Spring, even if it's only the brighter blue of the sky glimpsed through a lattice of television aerials.

But there will be so many more signs awaiting your pleasure — the drab privet hedges suddenly appear bright green; tubs and windowboxes which have been passed unnoticed for months suddenly sprout colourful displays. Birds everywhere don their courting plumage, and are perkier than ever.

Spring is definitely here — it costs nothing, and there's nothing to stop you enjoying it!

SATURDAY—APRIL 10.

EMMA is a nurse at a hospital not far from us. We always admire her, what she has done and is continuing to do with her life. When she is not working she is involved with the Girl Guides, her nursing association, reading and handicrafts. She is always busy caring for people.

Whatever their state of health, nursing the elderly is a challenge to Emma. She enjoys using her skills for long-term caring and has built up a satisfying rapport with many of her patients.

If you meet her, Emma may seem an ordinary person but the Lady of the House and I know that many people think she is very special. She loves and serves others without any thought of reward.

SUNDAY—APRIL 11.

FOR I have given you an example, that you should do as I have done to you.

John 13:15

MONDAY—APRIL 12.

I LIKE the story of the teacher in a Yorkshire classroom who asked her class, "Who can tell me which animals are peculiar to the Arctic regions?"

Like a flash, Jimmy replied, "Lions, tigers and elephants."

When she asked the reason for his reply Jimmy, with impeccable logic, replied, "Well, wouldn't *you* think it peculiar if you saw them there?"

BIRDS'-EYE VIEW

TUESDAY—APRIL 13.

ENVY

*THE nightingale gazed at the peacock
  And wished with all its might:
"If only I had feathers
As lovely and as bright!"*

*But that night in the darkness
The listening peacock sighed:
"Why can't I sing as sweet as that
Small brown bird?" it cried.*

Maurice Fleming.

WEDNESDAY—APRIL 14.

I WONDER if you have ever heard the story about the farmer on his way to market whose cart suddenly overturned into a ditch and was wrecked?

A little crowd, including an elderly man, soon gathered round expressing their deepest sympathy. It appeared that there was nothing at all to be done, until the man stepped forward and, handing the farmer some coins, said, "I'm sorry five guineas."

Then turning back to face the crowd he said, "Friends, how much art thou sorry?"

The message of the story is that it is always good to express our sympathy and concern in words when somebody is in trouble — but it is very much better to offer some practical help as well!

THURSDAY—APRIL 15.

READING the autobiography of the actor Peter Cushing, we learn that as a boy he always wanted to be an actor, and years later the shy young man was to achieve his heart's desire.

Life was far from easy for him. He had to contend with long periods of ill health, both his own and his wife, Helen's, and this meant no work — living in poverty with no real home. During these spells he found that he had a talent for making jewellery and painting scarves, and fortunately managed to sell them to keep the wolf from the door.

Peter Cushing concluded: "There is a divinity that shapes our ends." As we live through both the rough and the happy times of life, we, too, should remember this.

FRIDAY—APRIL 16.

PASSING a cosmetic display in a big store the Lady of the House once found herself pondering the words of a member of a religious order who, when asked which cosmetics she used, gave this recipe:

"For my lips I always try to use truth; for my eyes, pity; for my hands, charity; for my figure, uprightness; for my heart, love. I can't always get them in the right proportions," she added, "but I do try."

And to try is the most beautiful quality of all, as I'm sure you'll agree.

SATURDAY—APRIL 17.

MANY of us have learned the truth of that old adage: "Laugh and the world laughs with you; weep and you weep alone." We are told that laughing is not only a pleasant thing to do but is positively good for us, and that a good sense of humour can cure many of life's ills.

Writing in "Hope For The Troubled Heart", American evangelist Billy Graham said: "A keen sense of humour helps us to overlook the unbecoming, understand the unconventional, tolerate the unpleasant, overcome the unexpected and outlast the unbearable." Wise words, to be sure.

Last, but by no means least, a piece of wisdom from India reminds us that "the smile we send out returns to us."

SUNDAY—APRIL 18.

FOR God is the King of all the earth: sing ye praises with understanding.

Psalms 47:7

MONDAY—APRIL 19.

R L STEVENSON'S saying that "to travel hopefully is a better thing than to arrive" is well known. Much less familiar is the rest of the sentence which says: "and the true success is to labour".

That's just as worth remembering, isn't it? Keep it in mind today.

TUESDAY—APRIL 20.

IN his play "Waiting For Godot", the Irish writer Samuel Beckett has two tramps trying to pass the time as they sit by the roadside with nothing to do and nowhere to go. It's a play that means different things to different people, but for me it carries a powerful message — without a purpose in life we make no progress.

The road of life is for travelling, for pressing onwards and grasping opportunities along the way. If we lose interest, give up hope, we are stranded, like Beckett's tramps.

In the words of the song, we have to "Keep right on to the end of the road."

WEDNESDAY—APRIL 21.

AWAKE and sing at the day's first dawning,
Awake and sing, as you go your way,
Awake and pray with the first sweet music —
A blackbird sings on an April day.

Awake and smile, if the day is gloomy,
Awake to the knowledge God is good —
If there are clouds and mists in the valley,
Still there are daffodils in the wood.

Awake and feel all the warmth of friendship,
Friends, who are kindly, good and true,
Feel all the love and the prayers of that someone,
Kneeling a moment in prayer for you.
                                    Margaret Dixon.

STILL WATERS

THURSDAY—APRIL 22.

"COME to Helmsley," advertised the travel brochure, "and hear the legendary bells ring — but only during the daytime."

Apparently, the bells of All Saints Church ring out clearly during the day but between the hours of 11 p.m. and 6 a.m. they are muted, so that the town's residents and its guests can sleep in peace. The silencer was supplied by the owners of the nearby Black Swan Hotel who were especially concerned about their own guests' beauty sleep.

It was one of those thoughtful acts which can make such a difference to someone else's peace of mind — being a considerate neighbour, or taking the trouble to listen to someone with a problem.

Let's do all we can to make sure we don't spoil anyone's "beauty sleep" today.

FRIDAY—APRIL 23.

I ONCE caught sight of these words framed above a busy friend's desk:

"Just do today what today you should do, and today and every day will be good days for you."

SATURDAY—APRIL 24.

FROM across 500 years comes this advice from Thomas À Kempis:

"Never be entirely idle, but be either reading, or writing, or praying, or meditating, or endeavouring something for the public good."

Wise words never go out of date, do they?

SUNDAY—APRIL 25.

APPLY thine heart unto instruction, and thine ears to the words of knowledge.

Proverbs 23:12

MONDAY—APRIL 26.

WHENEVER the Lady of the House and I go shopping at our local supermarket, I always insist on pushing the trolley. Often I find one with a mind of its own. You know the kind I mean — they insist on going sideways, or when you push them to the right they promptly go to the left.

On a recent visit we bumped into the manager having a good laugh. "We're accused of playing all sorts of tricks to increase business," he said, "but this is the limit."

He had just been talking to an irate lady with an unmanageable trolley. "I know why you have them like this," she'd declared. "You have them programmed by computer so they always steer towards the dearest items."

No wonder the manager was laughing.

TUESDAY—APRIL 27.

THERE'S an old hymn which begins: "Have you had a kindness shown? Pass it on . . ."

Someone has pointed out that kindness is one of the most difficult things to give away, for it is usually returned.

But that's no reason for not trying, is it?

WEDNESDAY—APRIL 28.

YOU know, all great things once began as a thought — for example, Oxfam, Save The Children Fund, The Red Cross — so many worthwhile ventures, all created in the mind of someone like us. The thought came, it grew and grew, then later bloomed.

Don't discard the wonderful thoughts that come to you as you dream, for you may be the one through whom God is about to work miracles. Perhaps it will be a quiet miracle whose ripples will extend around you, your family, your neighbourhood — or you may start some great movement which will go on and on, long after your own lifetime.

Provided, of course, you follow up that thought with action.

THURSDAY—APRIL 29.

HORACE, the Roman poet who lived and died before the birth of Christ, wrote:– "He that fears his blotches may offend, speaks gently of the pimples of his friends."

Centuries-old wise words to remember and reflect on, don't you agree?

FRIDAY—APRIL 30.

HERE'S something to think about today: when things go wrong, please don't forget that rain from grey skies, not only sun from blue skies, is needed to make a beautiful rose.

May

THERE are so many kinds of courage — instantaneous, planned, enduring, much of it shown by ordinary people, like ourselves.

One of the most courageous stories I have read was of a tanker-driver whose heavy vehicle carrying tons of nitric acid, spun out of control while going down a steep hill. He deliberately drove off the road and crashed, because he knew that at the bottom of the hill was a village. He also knew that he risked his own life.

Fortunately, he managed to jump clear seconds before the cab plunged over the edge of the road. Of course, he couldn't have been sure of this when he made his courageous decision.

Yes, we never know when we'll be called on to live courageously, be it for the moment, a day, or longer. We do know, however, that within ourselves are resources of strength and energy ready to come to our aid when we most need them. It's a comforting thought, isn't it?

AND he saith unto them, Follow me, and I will make you fishers of men.

Matthew 4:19

REST AND BE
THANKFUL

MONDAY—MAY 3.

THE Lady of the House had an unexpected visitor one day. She was an old schoolfriend who usually goes to faraway exotic destinations for her holidays, so we were surprised to hear that this time she had decided to stay at home.

"I booked into a very good hotel," she said, "in my home town! They have wonderful cuisine and specialise in tours of the surrounding countryside, visiting a lot of towns and villages within a ten-mile radius. I never realised how much there is to see and learn about so near at hand."

Isn't this a lesson we could all keep in mind? There is so much to interest us in our immediate surroundings, if only we take the trouble to look.

TUESDAY—MAY 4.

LAUGHTER

WHAT a funny thing it is
    The fact that we can laugh,
And if we all did more of this
    We'd cut our cares in half.
There's nothing quite so cheering
    As a smiling, happy face,
One that's always laughing,
    Spreading joy around the place.
For when we laugh we seem to ease
    The tension and the strain,
We just let go, and feel refreshed
    To cope with life again.

Kathleen Gillum.

WEDNESDAY—MAY 5.

THE Cornish coast is beautiful, but it can also be very dangerous when a mist creeps up from the sea. I have read that women in the fishing villages when there was a heavy mist would sing hymns from the cliffs to guide their men in the small fishing boats safely home.

They would sing the first verse of the hymn and then stop. Suddenly, through the silence would come a comforting sound — it was the men singing the second verse to let their womenfolk know that they were safe. It is also said the faith of these women was so great that even when there was no reply and they knew their men were lost to the sea for ever, they were quite sure that their loved ones were safe with the Greatest of all Fishermen.

May we, too, venture forth in faith and, like these women, trust where we cannot see.

THURSDAY—MAY 6.

LOOKING at a clump of dandelions sprouting in the garden after a wet and warm spell, I was reminded of what an old countryman once said when I spoke about the weeds in a roadside verge.

"Weeds!" he said. "Do you think God would make weeds? These are wild flowers, His handiwork, and who are we to turn up our noses at 'em?"

Who, indeed?

FRIDAY—MAY 7.

WHEN I was young, I used to watch an old shepherd training his sheepdogs. As each dog returned to him he rewarded it with a biscuit, even if it had not done the job properly. One day I said, "I don't think you should give your dogs biscuits if they haven't succeeded in doing what you want."

"Oh, but you see, Francis," said my wise companion, "the biscuit is not given for succeeding — it is for trying."

A story worth remembering!

SATURDAY—MAY 8.

A FEW years ago I came across a thought-provoking article by a Mr D. Sen entitled "Where The Sun Shines". He did not praise a foreign country, but concentrated on our inner climate. His final paragraph read:

"Above all, remember you are trying to create a little sunshine where there was darkness . . . We need all the sunshine we can get."

We all appreciate "sunny" people, and feel happier to have met them. So it is up to us to join the "sunshine brigade" ourselves — even on the dullest day.

SUNDAY—MAY 9.

FOR who in the heaven can be compared unto the Lord?

Psalms 89:6

MONDAY—MAY 10.

CHRISTIAN AID is 50 years old this year and during the second week in May, volunteers will be starting their annual house-to-house collections.

Founded by the British Council Of Churches, it gives relief in emergencies and supports development programmes in health, agriculture and education in the poorest parts of the world. By giving even a small amount, we can contribute towards the cost of vaccinating children against disease or help to provide food for starving people.

Here is a prayer for Christian Aid Week which you may like to use as your own:

"Tender God, this Christian Aid Week teach us to open our eyes and hearts to see and feel the injustices which surround us. Let us learn to weep with the grieving, to embrace the outcast, to speak out for the silenced. Strengthen us so that we may act, in love and in celebration of the gift of life you offer to us all. May our lives become places of healing in your broken world."

TUESDAY—MAY 11.

A NOTICE at Ballindalloch Castle in Scotland, where there is a herd of cattle in the grounds, says:

Admission Free
Bull Will Charge You Later!

Visitors please take heed!

WEDNESDAY—MAY 12.

"THANK you for listening," said the voice at the other end of the telephone. "Not at all," I answered, feeling pleased but slightly embarrassed.

The Lady of the House and I knew that our friend Joan had many problems, and there often seemed to be little we could do to help. We offered advice whenever possible and made sympathetic replies when she poured out her troubles.

I began to wonder if we had underestimated the importance of all the phone calls. If there is nothing practical we can do for someone, then perhaps the next best thing is to let them talk. Listening may be just the help they need.

THURSDAY—MAY 13.

THREE-YEAR-OLD John loved to have his bath at Grandma's house because she still had some of the plastic ducks that his father used to play with. One day he went upstairs on his own, and all was so quiet that his grandmother soon went to investigate.

"Oh, John," she said reprovingly, "why have you broken up all my pretty little guest soaps?"

"I had to, Grandma," was the serious reply. "The ducks were hungry and I had to give them their supper."

There's no doubt that children have a logic all their own!

FRIDAY—MAY 14.

"GREAT oaks from little acorns grow." Yes, you know this saying, I'm sure, reminding us that even the biggest and most noble schemes and events each start in a small way — thus inspiring us to begin, in turn.

But there is another saying from the acorn and the oak which is, to my mind, even more thought provoking: "Today's mighty oak is yesterday's little nut that held its ground."

In other words — having made a start, stick to it — that's the only way to achieve your goal, and to attain satisfaction in the end.

SATURDAY—MAY 15.

I WAS passing a neighbour's house when I stopped to admire the beautiful flowers.

"It's all thanks to the birds," Helen explained.

She told me how she had retired the previous year and, as she now had more time, she had been feeding the birds all Winter. They didn't stop visiting the garden when warmer weather arrived, and for the first time in years her plants had not been ruined by insects.

Our little acts of kindness can often bring unexpected rewards, sometimes out of the blue.

SUNDAY—MAY 16.

FEAR God, and keep his commandments: for this is the whole duty of man.

Ecclesiastes 12:13

THE FRIENDSHIP BOOK

MONDAY—MAY 17.

I WOULD like to pass these thoughts from Esther Baldwin York on to you today:

"Life is a series of todays which so quickly turn into yesterdays that some of us spend our time looking regretfully backward. Still others, through worry or procrastination, are always waiting for tomorrow. In either case, there's the real danger of overlooking a very important day — today. For this is the place and the time for living. Let us live each day abundantly and beautifully while it is here."

I hope that we may all have a very good day!

TUESDAY—MAY 18.

L IKE most people I have my favourite coffee shop, somewhere I can sit and unwind as I refresh myself with that aromatic brew, and sometimes I can't help but observe the comings and goings of others.

If it's Tuesday I know they'll be there — the folk who perhaps make this particular coffee shop my favourite. A feeling of relaxation and contentment seems to radiate from their table, and touches upon all those fortunate to be sitting close by. They're obviously good friends, indeed old friends, and I wonder when and where they all first met.

Friendship like theirs gives pleasure not only to themselves, but also to anyone lucky enough to be around them.

WEDNESDAY—MAY 19.

IT was a lovely bright day and John and I were having a leisurely chat about many things over the garden wall.

"Isn't life a funny mixture of sweet and sour, Francis? I always used to fret and fume when things went wrong, and I experienced life's frustrations and pinpricks.

"But nowadays, I just try to count each day's sunny hours, a bit like that sundial over there near the lawn. Maybe it all depends on how you look at things, but surely if you count all the small successes and bright moments to be found each day, it's surprising just how many there are altogether. Life is a funny mixture indeed, Francis, but one which is often rather more sweet than sour."

How true that is!

THURSDAY—MAY 20.

THE TINY FLOWER

A TINY flower bent low its head,
"I am not pretty, Lord," it said,
"I simply drink the morning dew,
And say a little prayer to You."

But, when a sad heart saw the flower,
It seemed to fill the lonely hour
With comfort and with gentle Grace.
A tiny flower — in God's own place.

Margaret Dixon.

THE FRIENDSHIP BOOK

FRIDAY—MAY 21.

SOME time ago I heard a radio programme about Richmal Crompton who wrote the "Just William" books. It was mentioned that William had a favourite song: "Dare to be a Daniel, dare to stand alone . . ."

Actually, this was not a song, but a chorus often sung in Junior Temperance Society gatherings throughout Britain in the mid-1930s. The speaker remembered singing it with friends every Thursday evening.

Standing up for what you believe to be right is perhaps needed nowadays more than ever. Sometimes it certainly means adapting Daniel-like qualities.

SATURDAY—MAY 22.

MIKE works with deprived youngsters on a housing estate. It's his job to help them strive towards better things. How does he do it?

"It's hard going," he admits, "but when one of them says to me, 'I'll never make it, not coming from my background', I reply, 'It's not where you come from that matters, it's where you're going!' "

Good advice for us all, surely.

SUNDAY—MAY 23.

FOR whosoever shall do the will of my Father which is in heaven, the same is my brother, and sister, and mother.

Matthew 12: 50

MONDAY—MAY 24.

TURNING to a book is often a good idea when you're feeling a little down-hearted. One of my favourites is H.V. Morton's "In Search Of England," and the chapter that particularly impresses me is when the author meets an old clergyman living in a country area. "Happiness," remarked the man, "is a compound of simplicity, love and philosophy — and, of course, faith!"

After staying at the vicarage overnight Morton learned more about his new friend's philosophy. "We are happy because we have rarely known discontent."

Surely this is a message for modern times? We probably all realise this, but sometimes circumstances make us forget. That is, until we remember to be thankful for the good things we do possess, instead of worrying about the things we don't!

TUESDAY—MAY 25.

MY friend Bill met a former colleague, Elizabeth. She said, "We were sorry when you left. You added such a lot to our team."

After thanking her for the comment he walked on with lighter steps. A little appreciation — even years afterwards — still brings a glow of satisfaction. But how often we are slow to speak such words. Sometimes we even leave them unsaid — quite unintentionally — until it is too late to encourage the deserving one.

Don't leave words of praise unsaid.

WEDNESDAY—MAY 26.

MANY railway preservation societies arrange to run steam engines for nostalgia on special open days.

When steam trains were a regular form of transport, my mother used to say that an engine's motto when climbing a steep incline was: "I think I can, I think I can, I think I can." After reaching the top, the message changed to: "I knew I could, I knew I could, I knew I could!"

A good saying to remember when life is proving difficult for us, isn't it?

THURSDAY—MAY 27.

THERE is nothing we enjoy more than a walk in the country. Professor G. M. Trevelyan, the well-known historian, was an enthusiastic walker and a great supporter of the Youth Hostel Association. He once said, "I have two doctors — my left leg and my right."

Alfred Wainwright was another dedicated walker. He produced a series of guides and detailed maps to the Lakeland fells, and his television programmes brought spectacular scenery within reach of thousands. His sixth book contained this dedication:

"To those unlovely twins, MY RIGHT LEG and MY LEFT LEG, staunch supporters that have carried me about for over half a century, endured much without complaint and never let me down."

If we have a good pair of legs that can get us about, then we have much to be thankful for.

FRIDAY—MAY 28.

SHORTLY before the end of term when a class was about to move on to a new school, a teacher asked the pupils what they hoped to be in the future. There were the usual aspirations — well-paid jobs as airline pilots, scientists, doctors or pop stars, as well as the girl who was determined to marry a millionaire. One pupil, though, had remained quiet and thoughtful.

"What about you, Rosemary?" asked the teacher.

"I should like to be happy," she replied.

It is good that there are still youngsters who are aware of such values.

Aristotle Onassis, the Greek shipping magnate, was once asked what he wanted to possess but hadn't achieved. His reply was, "Peace of mind."

So, as we reflect on what is worthwhile, let's remember that the best things in life are — and always have been — free!

SATURDAY—MAY 29.

AFTER severe troubles and illness the famous flute-player James Galway decided that all his struggles to regain his health and career had taught him a lesson.

He is quoted as saying: "I decided henceforth I would play every concert, make every recording, as though it were my last."

We can't all be world-famous flautists, but we can adapt the motto to everyday living doing the best we can in life and work, day by day.

SUNDAY—MAY 30.

FOR the kingdom of God is not in word, but in power.

Corinthians I 4:20

MONDAY—MAY 31.

WHEN Lucy Ching was a baby she lost her sight. At that time, in China, blind people were thought to bring bad luck, so they were not educated and seldom even taken outside their homes.

However, Lucy was a determined child. When she was eight she heard that in some countries blind people could be taught and trained for employment, so she asked her brother, a radio ham, to appeal for information. A doctor in the Philippines heard the broadcast and sent a package of Braille. With that, she proceeded to teach herself to read and write.

Next, she fought to be admitted to school to be taught with sighted children. It was difficult, for she had to work long hours after school to press out her own Braille notes on newspaper. Yet in most subjects she came near the top.

She gained a scholarship for training in America, and now she is employed as a social worker with disabled people in Hong Kong.

Lucy Ching often used to say, "A blind person is an ordinary person who cannot see." Her work for the less fortunate in Hong Kong has made it possible for people, who thought they had no future, to follow in her footsteps.

June

CAPABILITY BROWN, the world-renowned 18th-century landscape gardener, designed the gardens of some of England's greatest and most attractive estates.

There is a story of how a friend was walking arm-in-arm with him in one of the gardens they had known before he altered it.

"I do hope that I go to Heaven before you do, Mr Brown," she said.

"Why, madam?" he asked.

"Because," came the reply, "I want to see what it is like before you get there to alter it!"

He was both astonished and moved by the thought, then realised at that moment just what he had been able to give to others. Generosity does not mean just sharing our money — it means sharing our talents, too.

GOD bless all optimists! Among these I would number the American poet Walt Whitman who wrote: "Life is more wonderful than one can suppose, and different."

A lovely way of looking at it.

THE fifth-form pupils from our local school were in the Lake District for their annual geography field study. The day chosen to climb Helvellyn and walk on Striding Edge dawned bright and sunny; everybody enjoyed the challenge to reach the top — and then it happened . . .

When they looked down at the panoramic view, a boy called Philip became paralysed with fear of heights. He felt so ashamed of his vertigo as his teacher gradually guided him back down the mountain.

That evening the teacher concerned explained to his pupils how a Swiss climbing friend of his had said that the only cure for this type of giddiness is to help someone else more frightened and in even greater difficulty. Practice may not lead to a complete cure, but forgetfulness of self can achieve it.

SING a song of living,
And render it each day
With hopeful notes by giving
  Commitment come what may.
A Great Conductor's waiting,
  And his function seems to be
To lead us in creating
  Universal harmony.
          J. M. Robertson.

SATURDAY—JUNE 5.

ANNA has always been a great one for getting straight to the point, so I suppose I shouldn't have been too surprised when she told me that her favourite prayer consisted of only one sentence.

"How does it go?" I asked with some curiosity.

She closed her eyes. "Dear Lord, throughout each day, help me to remember You, and to forget me." Then she looked up and smiled at me. "I know it's very simple, but I think it says a lot, don't you?"

I agreed. So often it is only when we have stopped thinking about our own needs and wishes that we are able to find true fulfilment in serving Our Lord.

SUNDAY—JUNE 6.

JESUS saith unto him, Rise, take up thy bed, and walk.

John 5:8

MONDAY—JUNE 7.

MANY of us, who love books and reading, will agree with these words from the 18th-century writer, Oliver Goldsmith, who wrote that well-known classic "The Vicar Of Wakefield":

"The first time I read an excellent book, it is to me just as if I had gained a new friend; when I read over a book I have perused before, it resembles the meeting with an old one."

Friends can come in many guises.

TUESDAY—JUNE 8.

ONE summer we had a visit from a friend who is a city dweller. The Lady of the House and I took James on our favourite walk along the canal towpath and it was very peaceful. As we paused to watch the shining water, he turned and said, "Listen!"

We obeyed, but heard nothing. Then he smiled and continued, "Silence — isn't it wonderful?"

Later, as he took his leave, James said he would cherish the memory of our walk. It would help him to face the noise and the bustle when he reached home. A few days later we received a card from him, which just said: "Thank you for the sound of silence. I carry it with me in my heart."

We wish our friend well, and all those who need a little peace to help them in their busy lives.

It seems that silence is golden, after all.

WEDNESDAY—JUNE 9.

WE can all admire someone who has risen to do great things in our country or community, and is in the public eye — especially if he or she remains humble about their achievements.

I like what George Thomas, one-time speaker of the House of Commons, said when he was asked about his promotion to the House of Lords — "I shall still be the same size in the bath!"

Lord Thomas believed in dignity without pomposity.

THURSDAY—JUNE 10.

IN Summer I often leave a little note on the kitchen table for the Lady of the House, if she is out. It will often say: "You'll find me in the garden."

Now, talking of gardens I rather like these lines by the English poet and writer Mary Howitt. She was born in 1799, and Mary and her husband William were well-known writers in their day.

Yes, in the poor man's garden grow
Far more than herbs and flowers —
Kind thoughts, contentment, peace of mind,
And joy for weary hours.

I repeated this quote to John, a friend of ours, who seems to have had more than his share of life's rough patches. When I finished, he nodded in agreement.

"You know, Francis, when I have problems and feel a bit downhearted, I like to go out and work in the garden. Maybe it is just being in the fresh air beside so many growing things, but I know I go back indoors more relaxed and hopeful about dealing with my worries, which seem to become smaller."

I smiled. "That's the value of your garden, John. Mary Howitt knew all about it, and so do lots of people, including yourself !"

FRIDAY—JUNE 11.

EVERY day is like a suitcase — some people pack more into it than others.

WHERE THE HEART IS

SATURDAY—JUNE 12.

THERE are many ways of wishing people well. One of my favourites is an old Eskimo blessing: "May you have warmth in your igloo, oil in your lamp and peace in your heart."

A simple wish that says it all.

SUNDAY—JUNE 13.

FOR in him we live, and move, and have our being; as certain also of your own poets have said, For we are also his offspring.

Acts 17:28

MONDAY—JUNE 14.

"LIFE is a great bundle of little things". I think there is more to these words of Oliver Wendell Holmes, the 19th-century American physician and writer, than first meets the eye.

Just think of the great bundle — the many little things in life, which give you pleasure. Perhaps you find delightful the sweet-smelling freshness of an early Summer morning, a diamond-bright Winter's day, the cheerfulness of daffodils in the shops in January, the feeling that you have helped someone, even if it is only in a small way. Or maybe the satisfaction of tackling successfully some of the little things in life, which you don't find so appealing, can give you quite a lift.

Chaucer wrote: "For the proverb saith that many small maken a great".

I think that most of us would agree with that.

TUESDAY—JUNE 15.

HELEN KELLER is perhaps the most famous blind and deaf person in history. Her other highly-sensitive abilities helped to make up for the lack of two important senses.

On one unforgettable occasion, she invited a member of the audience to play the music to which Joyce Kilmer's famous poem "Trees" was set. A young blind pianist came up and proceeded to play the tune. Helen stood with her hand on the piano lid — feeling the vibrations.

When it was all over, she thanked the pianist, saying, "The way you played that music, I could feel the sound of the leaves in the wind."

Helen Keller once advised: "Make the most of every sense" — and she certainly did!

WEDNESDAY—JUNE 16.

THE Lady of the House once saw a lovely cartoon. She cut it out and stuck it in one of her scrap books.

It showed an elderly couple sitting up in bed enjoying a cup of tea. The window was wide open. On the window-sill a sparrow was perched, its beak wide open and singing its heart out. The caption underneath read:

"Owing to the inclement weather there will be no dawn chorus this morning, but I hope you will accept this little solo in its place."

What a lovely sentiment! We can't all produce "a dawn chorus", but most of us could surely sing a little song to bring cheer to somebody.

THE FRIENDSHIP BOOK

THURSDAY—JUNE 17.

IT was the school sports day and ten-year-old Jon was running in his race. Unfortunately, he wasn't doing very well and one by one the other boys were overtaking him. His friends were watching and one said, "Jon needs a cheer!"

So they all called out, "Come on, Jon, you're catching up!" When he heard them, Jon took fresh heart and put on an extra spurt, outstripping his opponents, and was first past the winning post.

It's a lesson for life, I think. When difficult times come along it can make all the difference to know that we have friends beside us, encouraging us, wishing us well and doing all they can to help us to finish the race.

FRIDAY—JUNE 18.

IT'S strange how compliments are sometimes taken entirely the wrong way. When I met our friend Martha one day, she was looking very down in the mouth. It wasn't like her, for although she must be around 85 years old, she is usually as bright as a button and walks along like someone half her age.

"What's the matter?" I enquired.

"Oh, Francis, I've just been told I'm looking terribly well," Martha replied.

"You should be pleased!" I exclaimed.

"Not at all. When someone tells me that, I always suspect that they're surprised because they think I'm growing really old!"

You can't win!

SATURDAY—JUNE 19.

THE Lady of the House and I agree wholeheartedly with these words written by Ralph Waldo Emerson, the American essayist and poet, born in Boston in 1803:

"The ornament of a house is the friends who frequent it."

It is a sentiment with which I'm sure you'll agree.

SUNDAY—JUNE 20.

THE LORD preserveth the strangers; he relieveth the fatherless and widow.

Psalms 146:9

MONDAY—JUNE 21.

I AM always rather sorry when we reach the 21st of June, the longest day, because it reminds me that Winter will all too soon be here. At first the change is gradual, for the days draw in so slowly. Then suddenly, when the clocks go back, it gets so much darker earlier and Winter seems to have crept up on us unawares.

Isn't that just like the bad habits we have? They start being barely noticeable until something happens to trigger them off, then before we know it the habit is well and truly established, difficult to break.

We can't do anything about the shortening days, but we can certainly stop bad habits creeping up on us.

TUESDAY—JUNE 22.

I HAVE long been an admirer of the American writer, Henry David Thoreau, but I think my favourite quotation is the following:

"If a man does not keep pace with his companions, perhaps it is because he hears a different drummer. Let him step to the music he hears, however measured or far away."

I now have these words in a small frame and I read them often. They remind me, when I am tempted to be critical of others, that we all work in different ways, move at different speeds and all have a part to play in the great scheme of things.

If you have friends who are quiet, then treasure them. Never try to hurry them, for, in the bustle of our modern world, they are people worth knowing. Perhaps they, too, in their own way, step to a different drummer.

WEDNESDAY—JUNE 23.

I CAME across these helpful lines entitled "A Simple Code":

*No grumbling, no sulking, no feuding,
  no fighting,
But looking and looking for things to
  delight in!
No hating the state of the world every minute,
But seeking and finding the beauty that's in it.
No worrying and letting your troubles
  confound you,
But laughing and liking the people around you!*

THURSDAY—JUNE 24.

I LIKE the story told of the great Polish pianist Ignacy Jan Paderewski.

After one concert in which he had played, a gushing admirer came up to him and exclaimed, "Oh, Mr Paderewski, you must have had a world of patience to play like that!"

"Not at all," came the reply. "I have no more patience than anyone else, you know. It's just that I use mine."

FRIDAY—JUNE 25.

WINCHESTER Cathedral has a famous West Window. It is admired by thousands of visitors every year, yet it is nothing but a "hotch potch" of small pieces of glass put together in a haphazard way. It means a lot to the local folk, because it serves as a sad reminder that in the 17th century Oliver Cromwell almost overran the city.

Cromwell hoped, no doubt, to destroy the cathedral but all he did was to break up the beautiful West Window. Later, the good people of the town collected all the pieces of broken glass and used them to make a new whole. So although its original beauty has gone, the window now has a unique charm.

When life appears to be completely shattered, if we can make the effort to pick up the pieces and do our best to restore harmony, surely some good will, in time, emerge.

COASTAL CALM

SATURDAY—JUNE 26.

OLD Arthur was in the merchant navy all his working life, but now that his health is not always too good he has gone to live with his married daughter in a town many miles inland. The first time I went to visit him, he was missing the sea terribly and couldn't stop talking about his loss.

"I've had the sound of it in my ears for so long," he said, "I can't do without it."

The next time I called he was a different man. "Look," he said, "I've got the sea here whenever I want it."

He picked up a large seashell and cupped it over an ear. "My daughter brought me this," he beamed. "Wasn't that a wonderful idea?"

It certainly was.

SUNDAY—JUNE 27.

AND the glory of the Lord shall be revealed, and all flesh shall see it together: for the mouth of the Lord hath spoken it.

Isaiah 40:5

MONDAY—JUNE 28.

THESE wise words should give us plenty to ponder:

"Yesterday's dreams give us hope for tomorrow."

"Memories grow like flowers in the garden of life — tend them with care."

TUESDAY—JUNE 29.

HOW difficult it is to tell if a diamond is real or imitation. To us they all appear to sparkle equally brightly, especially when the sun shines on them. But there is a proven test — place a diamond in water and if it is worthless it will lose all its lustre. Put a true diamond in water and it continues to sparkle as brightly as ever.

Ah, you might say, I know some people like that — bright and sparkly when all goes well, but such "dreary moaning jimmies" when even a tiny dip in fortune overcomes them! Remember, stones can't change, but we, being humans, can. It's a comforting thought, and makes you begin to sparkle right away, doesn't it?

WEDNESDAY—JUNE 30.

SOME years ago when visiting Ripon Cathedral in North Yorkshire, I noticed an elderly man busy sketching in the nave. He smiled pleasantly when I stopped to admire his work and explained, "I'm not an artist by profession, just a retired postal worker."

Yet Jim Gott's sketches became well known, simply because he employed his talents so effectively after retirement. It is amazing how many men and women who have spent their working lives in "ordinary jobs" later discover previously-unknown talents such as painting, writing and playing music.

It is never too late to cultivate new talents.

July

DURING the Summer holidays the Lady of the House and I took a friend's young son to the circus. It was an evening performance, so everything seemed especially thrilling to the little fellow. As we watched Brian, his eyes were shining with excitement.

Later, on the way home, we asked him what he'd enjoyed most. Without a moment's hesitation he replied, "The clown, because he fell about so much. It must have hurt a lot, but he didn't cry."

I suppose we all like a clown. He seems so vulnerable and pathetic, yet his gentleness always enables him to triumph in the end. However often he falls, he will rise again — smiling.

A child can see, admire and copy this — and so should we!

FRIDAY—JULY 2.

YOU'VE had a quarrel with somebody? You know you're entirely in the right? Well, think again. A philosopher once wisely observed that no quarrel can last long if the fault is on one side only.

Make it up — today. You'll be glad you did!

SATURDAY—JULY 3.

OF course we can all admire a pair of beautifully-kept hands — white, elegant and slender. But even more beautiful, in my opinion, are hands which have been hardened and roughened by a lifetime of honest work.

Whenever I see hands like that I think of a line by the 19th-century American poet, James Russell Lowell: "Blessed are the horny hands of toil."

SUNDAY—JULY 4.

WHOSOEVER shall compel thee to go a mile, go with him twain.

Matthew 5:41

MONDAY—JULY 5.

*S*O live this day, that at its close
You may feel no shame, but gladness
At something you have done . . . or tried to do.

So live this day, that at its close
Someone may have cause to bless you
For something you have done . . . or tried to do.

So live this day, that at its close
You may rest in peace and quiet content
Knowing what you have done . . . or tried to do.

Try, that's the important thing. Remember that legendary spider, then like him — you will eventually make it!

THE FRIENDSHIP BOOK

TUESDAY—JULY 6.

I VISITED an acquaintance of ours, a young woman with three children. She had recently broken her leg, and my mission was to deliver a cake from the Lady of the House. As I was used to seeing Paula only in passing, and always in a hurry, I wondered how she was coping with her enforced inactivity.

She looked thoughtful. "Before my accident," she said, "I used to feel that if I was not always rushing around, then I must be wasting time. But now by having to sit still, I think I've learnt more in the last few weeks than I ever knew before. Not only have I found that my family can still cope, even if I don't run round after them, I've also discovered that just being a listener is important.

She smiled. "I hadn't realised that *being* around is sometimes more important than *rushing* around."

WEDNESDAY—JULY 7.

IN a shop I once noticed an attractive display of pictorial doormats — some with humorous comments, some patterned. All were arranged around a central mat with the one word "Welcome" on it.

The writer of the Letter to the Hebrews in the New Testament gives an overwhelming reason for writing "Welcome" on a mat. He said:

"Do not forget to entertain strangers, for by so doing people have entertained angels without knowing it."

THURSDAY—JULY 8.

THERE was no talking allowed in class during my schooldays. Our teachers never tired of sternly reminding us, "Empty vessels make most noise". I recalled this saying many years later when I read a little collection of quotations about conversation:

"Most of us know how to say nothing — few of us know when."

"There is only one rule for being a good talker — learn to listen."

"A wise man thinks all he says, a foolish one says all he thinks."

FRIDAY—JULY 9.

OLD Bert's garden is always a picture. He was working in it as usual the day before he went down with a serious illness. For a time it was feared he wouldn't pull through, but he amazed us all and when I passed his gate some time afterwards, there he was, hoeing his border as vigorously as ever.

I congratulated him on his recovery.

He grinned. "Well, Francis, it was the weeds that did it."

"The weeds?" I queried.

"Yes. When I was lying there, I suddenly thought, *they* never give up — so I won't, either!"

Bert's a fighter. Those weeds just don't stand a chance!

SATURDAY—JULY 10.

POSSIBLY you have been near the coast when a maroon has gone up. Certainly you will have seen the lifeboat, for it is always on view for all holiday visitors to see.

When the maroon goes off, then that boat is no longer just a big model to look at with admiration. It suddenly becomes the target for men from all around the town — the volunteer crewmen.

A gale may be blowing, mountainous seas foaming, a ship on the rocks, a holiday yacht capsized — the rescuers do not stop to count the cost. It is a moment of great danger, and they are urged on by the desire to help, to save lives.

We may not be called on to endanger our lives, but if we see someone needing a helping hand, a sympathetic ear, a word of comfort — we can be a "lifeboat", and rescue that person, from a different kind of storm.

SUNDAY—JULY 11.

BLESSED are the meek: for they shall inherit the earth.

Matthew 5:5

MONDAY—JULY 12.

WALT DISNEY, the great film maker, was a keen reader. He once said: "There is more treasure in books than in all the pirates' loot on Treasure Island. Best of all, you can enjoy these riches every day of your life!"

TUESDAY—JULY 13.

"ARE we disturbing you?" we asked our friend Mary when she invited us in.

"Not at all," she answered cheerfully, "I was just sitting and remembering. I do a great deal of that these days!"

She led us into her cosy sitting-room, which was filled with photographs and mementos of a long and busy life. As we shared a pot of tea, she told us some of the things she remembered and her words created pictures for us: Easter Weddings, Harvest Thanksgivings, snowball fights and summer picnics — we shared them all.

There was no mention of the unhappiness she had known, only the laughter and the love. As we were leaving, she urged us to visit her again and we promised that we would.

After all, "remembering" can be a very pleasant way of spending an afternoon — it did us as much good as it did for Mary.

WEDNESDAY—JULY 14.

HAVE you criticised anyone lately? You have? Yes, well, most of us do at some time or another. But on such an occasion please remember and think about these words from Oliver Goldsmith:–

"Blame where you must, be candid where you can,
And be each critic the good-natured man."

THURSDAY—JULY 15.

HENRY FORD, the American car magnate, was walking through his gardens with his great-grandson when the boy dropped something on the grass.

"What was that?" asked Ford.

"Only a penny," replied the youngster.

Without a word, the old man bent down and searched until he found the coin. Then he handed it back to the little boy who said, "Why did you stop to look for my penny?"

"My dear boy," replied Henry Ford, "if you were alone on a desert island, all the paper money in the world wouldn't do you any good — but think of a penny! It's metal — copper. You could hammer out a spearhead or use it as a tool. That penny is important, more important than paper money because you can use it for practical purposes. So don't drop a penny again!"

Something apparently insignificant can make all the difference in the world.

FRIDAY—JULY 16.

I ONCE read a wise observation, made by an elderly man who, to my mind, had grasped the true meaning of contentment:

"As you go along the road of life, hold fast to God with one hand, and open wide the other to your neighbour."

Just one sentence, but what a wealth of meaning in it.

SATURDAY—JULY 17.

REMEMBER, one thing is certain about the future — it will come one day at a time. Make the most of this one.

SUNDAY—JULY 18.

SALVATION belongeth unto the Lord: thy blessing is upon thy people.

Psalms 3:8

MONDAY—JULY 19.

THE little girl was entranced by the market stall and her mother couldn't understand it. Usually she looked at toys and books, games and clothes, but this was a haberdasher's display in the old tradition, selling the wide variety of goods Mum could only vaguely remember. There were buttons, and cottons a-plenty, bundles of lace and ribbon, needles and pins by the hundred.

Emily was too young to sew or embroider. Indeed, she still had trouble fastening buttons. After a while she said, "Mummy, could I have some ribbon, please? The colours are lovely."

Going home on the bus, the little girl took the sheaf of ribbons out of the paper bag.

"Look, Mummy," she said, "we bought a rainbow today!"

Her mother had never seen a rainbow in those colours, but did not say so. The delight of little Emily could not be spoiled. After all, rainbows are magical things, and who knows where and when we might find one?

TUESDAY—JULY 20.

MANY years ago, a lady called Sophie used to come to stay with friends in our village every Summer. She had spent most of her life in domestic service and appeared to lead a very quiet life in retirement. When she died, the Lady of the House and I accompanied several of her friends to the funeral, and we were amazed to see that the church was already quite full when we arrived.

After the service I was chatting to a neighbour and remarked how surprising it was that the service was so well attended. "Sophie might almost have been a famous film star!" I remarked.

"Oh, she was nothing like that," came the reply. "In fact, she was so quiet you'd hardly notice she was there, but she was one of God's little saints."

What a lovely epitaph that was!

WEDNESDAY—JULY 21.

HAVE you noticed that when we have had really bad weather in Winter, Summer sunshine is appreciated more than ever? It helps to cheer both our bodies and our souls.

At the seaside children laugh and play as the sea dances and sparkles in the sunshine, and even the people around us seem brighter and happier under the clear, bright skies.

How lovely life would be if we could keep this warm and sunny personality all year round. It certainly isn't easy sometimes to feel happy and bright when clouds are in the sky, but we can surely try.

THE FRIENDSHIP BOOK

THE best sermon ever preached was also one of the shortest. We have John Wesley to thank for it and here it is:

> *Do all the good you can,*
> *By all the means you can,*
> *In all the ways you can,*
> *In all the places you can,*
> *At all the times you can,*
> *To all the people you can,*
> *As long as ever you can.*

It says it all, doesn't it?

HARRY and I were at school together. We lost touch for many years and by the time I met him again he was the boss of a huge company. When I walked into his office I expected him to be . . . well, grim and rather self-important. Not at all. He greeted me with the grin I remembered so well.

As we chatted, my eye was caught by a framed verse on the wall. "That's my maxim," he told me. "I read it every morning before I start work." The verse was:

> *Give me a sense of humour, Lord,*
> *Give me the grace to see a joke,*
> *To get some happiness from life*
> *And pass it on to other folk.*

With a prayer like that in his heart, Harry will never go far wrong.

SATURDAY—JULY 24.

WHILE out one day, the Lady of the House and I decided that what we both needed most was a freshly-brewed pot of tea. We went into the nearest café and placed our order.

Imagine our surprise when the waitress returned — we each had been given a small teapot and even separate milk jugs. Somehow it wasn't quite the same. The atmosphere was gone.

It was only a small thing perhaps, but all the same a pleasure had somehow been lost, for what can be nicer than sharing a pot of tea and asking those time-honoured words: "Will I pour, or you?" Or sometimes nicer still is the phrase, "Will I be Mother?"

So, while we all have good-sized teapots at home, why not invite friends round to keep this simple pleasure going?

SUNDAY—JULY 25.

A WISE son heareth his father's instruction: but a scorner heareth not rebuke.

Proverbs 13:1

MONDAY—JULY 26.

HERE are a couple of thoughts worth keeping in mind today:

"Make the most of every day, and every tomorrow will hold a happy memory."

"Remember how to dream, for those who dream can touch the stars."

TUESDAY—JULY 27.

"YOU always seem happy and contented, yet you've not had an easy life at times," remarked a friend to an acquaintance.

"Well," she replied, "I try to remember the three S's! First of all, there's success. If you do something and fail, that's better than if you never try to do anything but succeed. Next, there's satisfaction. If you don't get everything you want, think of the things you don't get that you wouldn't want.

"Finally, there's serendipity. I'm lucky, for I often experience serendipity, the talent for making fortunate discoveries by accident. Oh, not great things, but simple pleasures and surprises."

It seems a good adage to remember.

WEDNESDAY—JULY 28.

A YOUNG friend took part in that age-old lesson — watching a seed germinate in water. Simon was thrilled. So, of course, the Lady of the House and I felt we had to experiment further, and into a glass jar we put a mixture of seeds ... beans, peas, radishes, cress.

And, as the tiny shoots began to grow and mix with one another in a fascinating pattern, I relived that sense of wonder I, too, had known as a child. It suddenly took on a new dimension — those different plants, growing together in an enclosed environment, seemed to be a model for our nation to follow today, a blend of different races, colours and creeds developing harmoniously side by side.

WAITING AND
HOPING

THURSDAY—JULY 29.

HERE are two sayings well worth keeping in mind today:

"The Lord is my lantern and I shall travel safely on the journey of my life."

"When all your tasks are finished, sleep well — God is awake."

FRIDAY—JULY 30.

SOME years ago, when the Duke of Norfolk was leading an M.C.C. cricket tour to Australia, he was the recipient of a presentation made by a young girl on behalf of a parish not far from Sydney.

Her parish priest had reminded her not to forget to say "Your Grace" when she handed the gift over to the Duke.

So it came to pass that the little girl presented the gift and said, "We hope you will accept this as a souvenir of your visit. For what we are about to receive, may the Lord make us truly thankful. Amen."

SATURDAY—JULY 31.

"OUCH! I've got a blister," exclaimed Tom, resting on a rake to rub his sore palm. He was doing a spot of much-needed tidying up in the local churchyard. Well, at least it could never be said of Tom: "Some folk are like blisters, they don't show up until the work is done!"

August

SEARCH the scriptures; for in them ye think ye have eternal life: and they are they which testify of me.

John 5:39

THE Lady of the House and I once spent a day at Cromer. At one end of the promenade we saw a delightful small statue.

It was a study of the face of a man in a sou'wester — Henry Blogg GC. BEM — the one-time coxswain of Cromer lifeboat, who had won an RNLI Gold Medal three times and a Silver one four times; all for conspicuous gallantry. He saved 873 lives in 53 years, with the help of his gallant crew.

His fellow townsmen say that he was one of the bravest men who ever lived. The people he saved would tell you that they had arrived safely ashore again because of the courage and skill of this faithful lifeboatman.

So, when things are hard going and difficult, think of Henry Blogg, exercise all your skill, put on a fine courage — and offer from your heart a prayer.

TUESDAY—AUGUST 3.

WHEN you get up, look out of the window and say to yourself, "I'm looking out at a brand-new day. It's never been used before and it will never be used again, so make the most of it and do the best you can with it."

Have a good day!

WEDNESDAY—AUGUST 4.

I ONCE read this saying and how true it is: Worry gives a small thing a big shadow!

Troubles may be very real and hard to forget, but we can surely tell the difference between these and fretting over trifles.

THURSDAY—AUGUST 5.

A SHOOT of wild honeysuckle once took root against my fence, a pretty little thing, so I decided not to disturb it. "You'll regret that," said one of my neighbours, "before you know where you are, it'll have taken over the whole border."

I'm sure Jim was right, but I didn't let that little plant have a chance to spread too far. I nurtured it, clipped it, trained it and it gradually grew into a thing of beauty. It was never an exotic specimen, but always remained its own simple and sweetly-scented self.

Friendships can be like my honeysuckle, can't they? They need to be nurtured and allowed to grow with a little love and consideration. Treat them well and they'll bring joy for a long time to come.

FRIDAY—AUGUST 6.

LET our words be happy words
  Of love and sympathy,
Let us speak of kindness
  And generosity.
Do not let unpleasant things
  Mar or spoil the day,
We should then think carefully
  Of what we're going to say.
For words can wound and injure,
  Or they can heal and bless —
So let us try to cultivate
  The words of happiness.

Kathleen Gillum.

SATURDAY—AUGUST 7.

I LIKE this definition of "happiness" and gladly pass it on to you: "Happiness is a perfume which you cannot pour on others without getting a few drops on yourself."

It tallies with something that La Bruyere once said: "The most delicious pleasure is to cause that of other people."

How true, don't you agree?

SUNDAY—AUGUST 8.

STAND in awe, and sin not: commune with your own heart upon your bed, and be still.

Psalms 4:4

MONDAY—AUGUST 9.

AN acquaintance in Belgium sent me an unusual saying to share: "A good devoter can never be a loser." In other words, anyone who devotes time to something will surely derive benefit from it.

The benefit gained may not be financial. Indeed, we may only feel a warm sense of achievement that a task has been successfully mastered. Or perhaps that help given to someone has made life a little brighter and easier.

Good words to remember.

TUESDAY—AUGUST 10.

WHEN daylight is fading, there is nothing I enjoy more than a last leisurely stroll round the garden to smell all the flowers whose perfume is best in the evening — for example, honeysuckle, night-scented stocks and evening primrose. It's something I can be sure will give me pleasant dreams!

As I savour the fragrance, I am reminded of all those friends who are getting on in years. Every experience has shaped their character and with the passing of time a growth in wisdom, tolerance, kindness and patience is quite noticeable.

So, in a philosophical turn of mind, I remember with thankfulness all those who have grown so fragrant in the evening of their lives — just like those lovely flowers in my garden!

WEDNESDAY—AUGUST 11.

IRIS HESSELDEN wrote these inspiring lines which tell you how to walk what she calls "The Path Of Peace":

> *Step light,*
> *And look for the sunshine.*
> *Grasp gently*
> *The kindness you find.*
> *Speak softly,*
> *And turn away anger.*
> *Sleep soundly,*
> *At peace with mankind.*
>
> *Walk proudly*
> *Through all your endeavours.*
> *Remember*
> *The battles you've won.*
> *Seek always*
> *The hope of tomorrow.*
> *Step lightly*
> *And look for the sun.*

THURSDAY—AUGUST 12.

IF you set out on a long journey you take maps with you, don't you? A guidebook is essential and perhaps even a compass.

What about life's journey? That great statesman, Winston Churchill, said he took with him large principles, a good heart, high aims and a firm faith.

They never let him down.

FRIDAY—AUGUST 13.

I WAS once listening to a discussion on the radio about bringing up children. Many theories had been put forward concerning food, routine, discipline and other matters. Finally, to wind up, the chairman asked each panellist to say what they considered to be the most important factor in bringing up a well-adjusted child. The final speaker had this to say: "To my mind by far the most important thing is that a child goes to bed naturally tired, but above all — happy."

A simple reply, perhaps, but like all seemingly simple statements it contained a profound truth — if a child can smile itself to sleep, there's little wrong in his or her life. And, for that matter, this applies to adults, too, doesn't it?

SATURDAY—AUGUST 14.

WHEN the sun shines for you, your personal sky is a beautiful blue, and all is well in your own little world, please remember those whose personal skies are cold and grey, and try to pass on to them a little of your sunshine.

It is wonderful how even a small kindness and a little caring can warm the heart.

SUNDAY—AUGUST 15.

A MERRY heart doeth good like a medicine, but a broken spirit drieth the bones.

Proverbs 17:22

MONDAY—AUGUST 16.

I LIKE the answer which a little girl gave to an Inspector of Schools when he visited her classroom in London. He had asked the children where they might see a large collection of beautiful pictures, hoping that someone might suggest The National Gallery. However, the youngster replied, "Please, sir, in my mind."

There are many pictures which the mind can conjure up — country scenes, rippling streams, trees with their fresh green leaves. Pictures of children or grandchildren, happy family occasions —holidays, birthdays, Christmases, and other special times . . . The list is endless.

By using the eye of the mind, unhurriedly, our lives can be enriched and no matter who we are, the pictures which seem to us most beautiful will be those in the mind.

TUESDAY—AUGUST 17.

WHAT I want to share with you today is a "find" I made at an antiques fair. Clocks and watches have always fascinated me, and I spotted a heavy, old-fashioned waistcoat pocket watch. The stall-holder opened the lid to let me read the inscription inside: "'Tis mine the passing hour to tell, 'tis thine to use it ill or well."

The couplet has remained imprinted on my mind. We all have the same number of hours in our day but how we use them, now, that's up to us, isn't it?

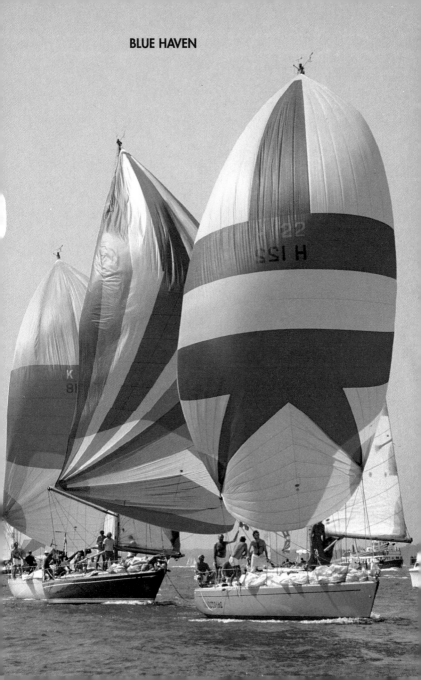

BLUE HAVEN

WEDNESDAY—AUGUST 18.

I READ the seaman's version of the 23rd Psalm not long ago and would like to share it with you today:

"The Lord is my Pilot. I shall not drift. He lighteth me across the dark waters; He steereth me in the deep channels; He keepeth my log. He guideth me by the star of holiness for His name's sake. Yea though I sail amidst the thunders and tempests of life, I shall dread no danger, for Thou art with me. Thy love and Thy care, they shelter me. Thou preparest a harbour before me in the homeland of eternity; Thou anointest the waves with oil; my ship rideth calmly. Surely, sunlight and starlight shall favour me on the voyage I take, and I will rest in the port of my God forever."

THURSDAY—AUGUST 19.

ELLEN ANN WILLMOTT was an Edwardian lady with a passion for gardening and plants. Her home was at Warley Place in Essex which once belonged to the diarist John Evelyn.

Her great interest was in collecting and propagating rare and beautiful plants, and she endeared herself to friends by a charming practice. When she paid them a visit, she took with her one of her "special collection" and planted it in a secret corner, to be discovered by her hosts with surprise and delight at some future date.

How fortunate we are if we have friends like Miss Wilmott who refresh us during their visits — and leave nothing but fragrance behind.

FRIDAY—AUGUST 20.

YOU all know that I love books, but I admit they do tend to overflow from my bookshelves into various other unoccupied spaces in our home; in fact, they seem to mysteriously, but delightfully, increase in number.

"When, Francis," the Lady of the House said to me the other day, "are you going to tidy your books? Perhaps you might have a few books for the church sale next week."

"Oh, I have been thinking about it," I replied.

Quick as a flash, the Lady of the House said to me, "You'll never plough a field by turning it over in your mind!"

Later, I did find some books for the church sale, and I hope whoever buys them will enjoy them as much as I did!

SATURDAY—AUGUST 21.

WE hear all sorts of theories about education nowadays. I think Thomas Huxley got it right when he said: "The most valuable result of education is the ability to do the thing you have to do, when it ought to be done."

SUNDAY—AUGUST 22.

AND it shall come to pass in the last days that the mountain of the Lord's house shall be established in the top of the mountains, and shall be exalted above the hills.

Isaiah 2:2

NATURE'S GLORY

MONDAY—AUGUST 23.

ONE of the crazes to hit America in recent years is the slogan "Practise Random Kindness And Senseless Acts Of Beauty". People are using it as stickers on cars, letterheads, newspaper adverts and notice boards in shops and offices.

As the use of the slogan spreads, so do the random acts of kindness — car washing or shopping for a neighbour, sitting with a housebound person or planting bulbs along the roadside. All these create beauty and help to lift the spirits of others.

It is one of those "catching" things and brings to mind some lines which I came across some time ago:—

A vision without a task is a dream,
A task without a vision is drudgery,
A vision with a task is the hope of the world.

TUESDAY—AUGUST 24.

OUR friend Alice, who lives a few streets away, told me that her young niece once had a tantrum and was sent to her room in disgrace.

Some time later she emerged with a letter for her mother. It said: "Dear Mummy, I hate you. All my love, Gemma."

Alice told me that Gemma's expression of love soon helped to restore domestic harmony that day!

THE FRIENDSHIP BOOK

*I HAVEN'T time, I'm rather busy, perhaps I will
if I'm free.*
*My work, my home, my garden need me,
I'll really have to see.*
*One day I might think about it, when I'm older,
then I will.*
*For the present I can't do it, some time later,
not until.*
*I don't think you need me really, I have such a
lot to do.*
*Someone else can do it somehow, it doesn't matter
who.*
*If I had a bit more money, if I had some time
to spare . . .*
*One day it will be convenient, one day, sometime,
perhaps next year.*
But — please don't think that I don't care.

This was written by Peter Tongman and though
its message was orignally intended for evangelism,
it can also be applied to so many things in life.
If we feel there is a good cause or a person we
know who needs our support — let's act now.

HUDSON TAYLOR, the great missionary,
once said of his work: "I used to ask God to
help me. Then I asked if I might help Him. I
ended up by asking Him to do His work through
me."

Isn't this a great example to follow?

FRIDAY—AUGUST 27.

NOT all children are interested in autograph books, but when our young friend Morwenna was given her grandmother's autograph album she was so thrilled. She brought it across to show to us and there was a lot of sound advice to be found on the pages. The saying which the Lady of the House and I liked best was simple and sincere. It read:

"Good, better, best, may you never rest till your good grows better and your better best."

SATURDAY—AUGUST 28.

AMONG the many wise sayings attributed to President Abraham Lincoln is this one: "Some men are like the stump the old farmer had in his field — too hard to uproot, too knotty to split, too wet and soggy to burn." Some neighbours asked him what he would do in a case like that.

"Well now, boys," he replied, "like the old farmer did, I should just plough around it."

Lincoln had decided that was a good way to deal with the difficult people we encounter in life — you can usually find a way round them if you look long enough.

SUNDAY—AUGUST 29.

BLESSED be he that cometh in the Name of the Lord.

Psalms 118:26

HORSE POWER

MONDAY—AUGUST 30.

HIGH up in Edinburgh Castle stands the tiny chapel built for Queen Margaret of Scotland. Margaret's charm and kindliness won not only the heart of her husband, King Malcolm, but of the Scottish people as well. She cared personally for nine orphan children, and each day saw to the needs of the poor who came to her door and who revered her as a saint.

There is a nice custom in St Margaret's Chapel. Fresh flowers are placed on the altar there to honour her — arranged by one of a guild of ladies, all named Margaret.

Like each of us, great or small, the memory of this lady is kept alive by her example and deeds.

TUESDAY—AUGUST 31.

OUR friend Peter is what most of us would call a trifle accident prone, or maybe he is simply a mite clumsy — things crumble and tumble, break and seem to develop minds of their own, when he is nearby. The latest minor catastrophe had left the garden shed handle in Peter's hand, and the shed's key jammed in that door's lock!

Peter looked at me with a rueful smile. "Francis, when this kind of thing happens I just say to myself, blessed are those who can laugh at themselves for they will have a source of ceaseless amusement." Then he added with a twinkle in his eye, "And so will others!"

A little humour and a smile can go a long way to lighten life's trials and tribulations!

September

WHEN Elsie decided to move into a ground-floor flat, she was very happy with everything except for the fact that her kitchen window looked out onto a dull brick wall.

"I shall have to do something about that," she said to herself. "I need something bright to look at when I'm doing the washing-up."

So she had the wall painted white and against it she put tubs which she had planted with the most colourful flowers she could think of — marigolds, geraniums, petunias and nasturtiums — and then she settled down to enjoy the transformation.

It isn't possible for us all to live in a delightful country cottage with roses round the door, but we can all do something to improve our situation. It's what we do with what we have that's important.

A LINGUIST was once asked which of all the many languages she had studied she considered the best.

She paused, thought for a moment and then answered, "The greatest language in the world is the language of love."

FOLLOWING THE PATH

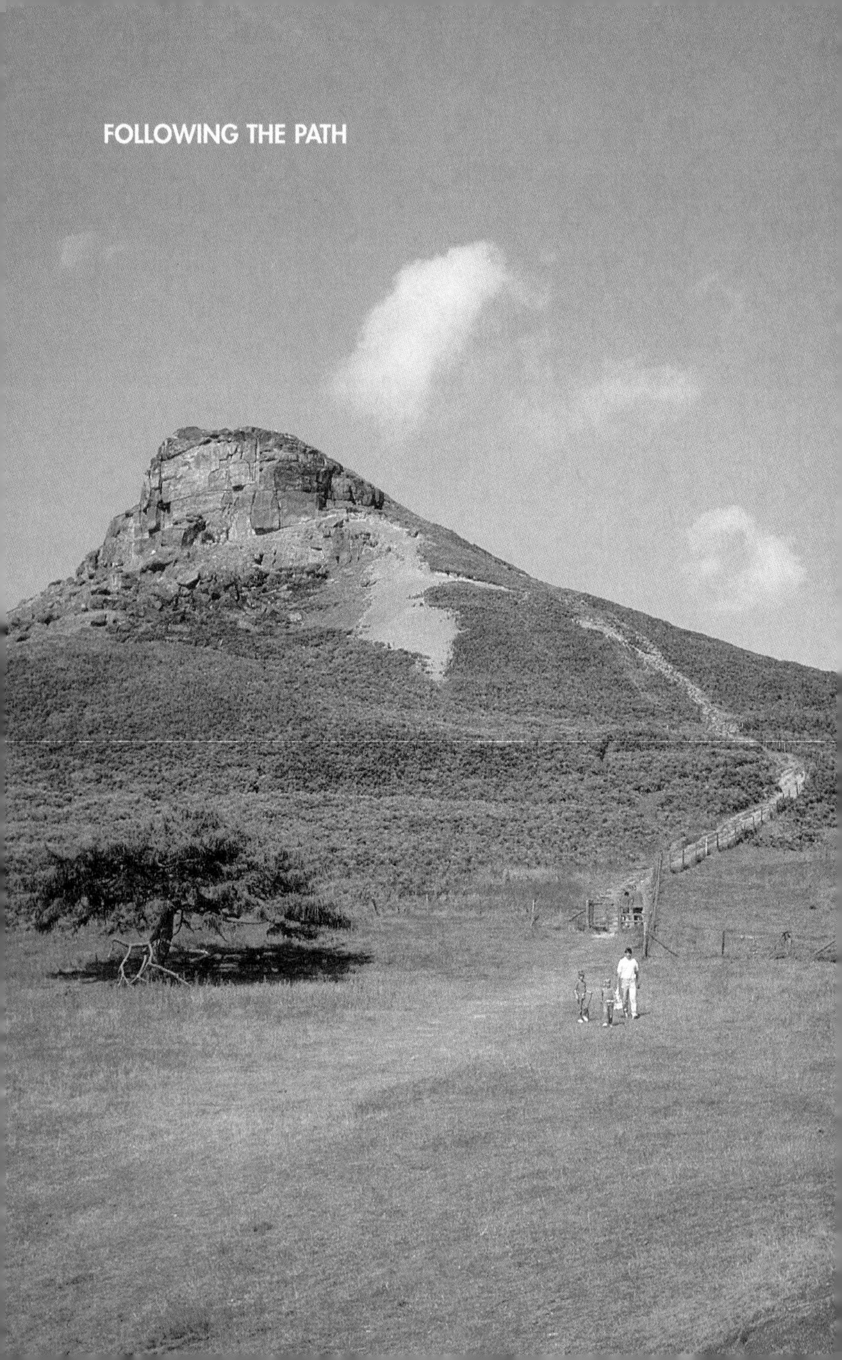

FRIDAY—SEPTEMBER 3.

LEAFING through an old book of poems, I came across these lines which I'd like to pass on to you:

LOOK ON THE SUNNY SIDE

Some people only see the world
As through a smoky glass,
They go halfway to meet the woe,
And let the sunshine pass.

Look always on the sunny side,
Twill make us happier far,
Why should we try to find the cloud,
When brightly shines the star?

SATURDAY—SEPTEMBER 4.

OUR friend Mary had a bit of a problem. It was nothing serious, you know, just rather a tiresome matter.

"But I *will* solve it, Francis, sooner or later," she said. "When something like this happens, I always remember the Brazilian saying which I once heard — 'There must be a little way' — and there usually is, if you think long and hard enough about it."

When I next saw Mary, she said with a smile, "I found my 'little way', Francis, you know, so my problem is now solved. I always remember Dr Samuel Johnson's wise words: 'It is by studying little things that we attain the great art of having as little misery and as much happiness as possible'."

SUNDAY—SEPTEMBER 5.

BEHOLD, children are a heritage from the Lord.

Psalms 127:3

MONDAY—SEPTEMBER 6.

I WONDER if, like me, you like to watch the weather forecast on television? It's such a help to try to know in advance if we are likely to need an umbrella or an extra warm coat when we venture outdoors!

Sometimes we are warned that there is a cold front on its way and we can expect to see unsettled, dull, cool or stormy days. Or it may be good news with fair, warm and settled days in store for us.

How very much like people, surely. I do hope that today the folk you and I come across will be the sunny and fair ones — not the cold and stormy ones. It can make all the difference!

TUESDAY—SEPTEMBER 7.

I CAME across these quotes, and I'd like to pass them on to you today:

"Happiness is sharing whatever we have, with someone we care for."

"Remember how to laugh — laughter is a tonic for the soul."

"Memories are priceless. Store carefully — handle with love."

WEDNESDAY—SEPTEMBER 8.

THE Lady of the House and I were invited to the harvest service at our local school one year to hear the songs, music and drama performed so beautifully by the infants.

"Bread" was the apt theme, and during the morning the village baker had been into school and had made bread rolls and bread mice with curly tails, helped by the pupils in the older classes, and they were displayed with all the other harvest produce.

As the children demonstrated using large cardboard letters, the word "harvest" also contains the letters making up sea and earth, and we reflected on all the fruits of sea and earth. But "harvest" also contains the letters that make up share, and at the end of the service the pupils distributed the bread they had made to parents and friends symbolising the sharing of the harvest.

It brought to mind something said by Mahatma Gandhi: "Earth has enough for every man's need but not for every man's greed."

THURSDAY—SEPTEMBER 9.

I ONCE came across this quotation from the French philosopher Albert Camus, and it greatly appeals to me. I hope you'll like the sentiments, too:

"Don't walk before me, I may not follow; don't walk behind me, I may not lead; just walk beside me and be my friend."

Who could resist such an invitation?

A TOUCH OF
TRANQUILLITY

THE FRIENDSHIP BOOK

FRIDAY—SEPTEMBER 10.

I ONCE read a biography of Thomas Edison the inventor. When he wanted to make a nickel iron-alkaline battery, I found that he performed fifty thousand experiments, and failed fifty thousand times. Someone who knew about this asked if all these failures had disappointed him.

"Not at all," replied Edison, "for I have learned fifty thousand ways it cannot be done, and therefore I am fifty thousand times nearer the final experiment!"

He, of course, eventually did succeed.

We all know that Edison was a genius, but when you think about it the greater part of his genius was because he never gave way to disappointment. He used his setbacks to lead him to success.

SATURDAY—SEPTEMBER 11.

THE ladies in St Anne's Parish Church congregation near Blackburn will no doubt be entitled to sympathy if they are heard to remark that they have "got a stitch", for they made an embroidered panel which depicts the life and times of the community, church and town.

It took thirty ladies all of seven years to do the work — 2,166,528 stitches in total. At the start it must have seemed daunting, but now the completed eighteen feet by six feet mural dedicated by the Bishop of Blackburn is displayed in the church for everyone to admire.

Isn't it wonderful what can be achieved when we have the same goal and everyone pulls together?

SUNDAY—SEPTEMBER 12.

FOR I know that my redeemer liveth, and that he shall stand at the latter day upon the earth.

Job 19:25

MONDAY—SEPTEMBER 13.

ONE evening, we had a power failure and were without electricity for a few hours. We drew back the curtains to let in as much light as possible, and sat beside the window watching the darkening sky.

It was most peaceful without television or radio, but it wasn't long before we were thinking about a cup of tea and would we be able to make toast in the morning? Then there was the fridge defrosting, and . . .

Shortly before midnight, we decided to go to bed — and then the lights came on! It was wonderful and made us realise how people must have felt years ago when electricity was first installed. They must have thought it a miracle after paraffin lamps and gas lighting. Just another example of those everyday things we take for granted.

TUESDAY—SEPTEMBER 14.

SOME people are full of talk about all the things they are going to do. When I hear somebody like that, I remember the old saying my grandfather taught me: "Brag is a good dog but Holdfast is a better one."

THE FRIENDSHIP BOOK

WEDNESDAY—SEPTEMBER 15.

*WAS it just coincidence
 When help was sent to me?
Did it happen just by chance,
 Or was it meant to be?*

*Was there an unseen helper
 Who planned the timely deed,
Who knew my situation,
 Who saw and met my need?*

*I do not know the answer,
 But strange it seems to be
That when I need a helping hand
 Assistance comes to me.*

Kathleen Gillum.

THURSDAY—SEPTEMBER 16.

I READ a story of how a woman once found a boy crying on a railway station platform. She found that he had lost his ticket.

She knew that she had to do something about it, so she bought him a ticket. It was given on one condition — that when the boy grew up and found somebody else in trouble he would try to help, too.

As the train moved off, the young traveller leaned out of the window and shouted, "I will pass it on, I promise!"

So if someone shows us a kindness in any way — remember this story. It is meant to be passed on.

FRIDAY—SEPTEMBER 17.

STRADIVARIUS, with his two sons, made world-famous violins, violas and cellos in their Italian workshop in Cremona 250 years ago. They are still much sought after today.

It is said that when Stradivarius went out to select wood for his instruments, he chose the part of the tree that had faced north. That was the side which had been buffeted by wind and weather — and withstood it — because that side of the tree, declared Stradivarius, gave the sweetest music.

How like life, I thought. So often we find that the people whose lives have been touched by hardship and sadness are somehow strengthened in the process, and seem to develop that extra depth of character which can be such a blessing to others.

SATURDAY—SEPTEMBER 18.

WOULD you like to be the perfect "good neighbour"? This anonymous verse tells exactly how!

Good neighbours are the sunshine of the morning,
  The comfort in the ordinary days.
Not the kind who are intrusive or demanding,
  Just there to share your life in quiet ways.

Ready with a smile or friendly greeting,
  A little gossip or some sweet surprises,
For therein lies the joy of daily living,
  Good neighbours, near at hand when need arises.

SUNDAY—SEPTEMBER 19.

USE hospitality one to another without grudging.

Peter I 4:9

MONDAY—SEPTEMBER 20.

ONE evening I had just put another log on the fire, picked up my pen, and settled down at my desk, when I caught sight of these words by Robert Louis Stevenson. Do you know them?

"To be honest, to be kind — to earn a little and to spend a little less, to make upon the whole a family happier for his presence, to renounce when that shall be necessary and not be embittered; to keep a few friends, but those without capitulation — above all, on the same grim condition, to keep friends with himself — here is a task for all that a man has of fortitude and delicacy."

Surely words which give those of us who read them much to think about!

TUESDAY—SEPTEMBER 21.

WHEN Miss Winton retired after many years of teaching, someone said to her, "You must feel very proud when you hear of clever pupils who have gone on to do great things."

"Yes," she said, "but the ones I am most proud of are those who were not at all bright academically but have found jobs, made good marriages, and are living quiet, decent lives. They are my star pupils!"

THE FRIENDSHIP BOOK

ONE of my favourite radio programmes is "Desert Island Discs", and some time ago I heard that great American soldier, Norman Schwarzkopf, telling the presenter of his real commitment to his job.

"Not just being involved," he said, "but being totally committed. There is a difference, you know. Think of the bacon and egg breakfast. The chicken was involved, but the pig committed."

As well as making me chuckle, it started me thinking about his words when I was weeding in my garden later that morning.

"Come on, Francis," I told myself, "this job calls for total commitment, not just general involvement!"

THESE days, have you noticed the ways in which people are counted as numbers on a computer? In so many senses we seem to be losing some sense of personal identity. Even in hospitals it can be so easy for doctors and nurses to refer to patients as a "heart" or a "gall bladder".

The Christian doctor Paul Tournier once said: "If I forget my patients' names, and remember them by a bed number, or by their ailment, the personal touch is gone, and the relationship between doctor and patient goes wrong."

So, when you hear statistics recording people, remember that they are real flesh and blood folk — not just a number — a loved one to somebody.

FRIDAY—SEPTEMBER 24.

WHEN young Philip's mother goes shopping, he likes to come and spend an hour or two with us. Often he brings his own toys and amuses himself indoors, but when the weather is fine, the Lady of the House and I like to walk with him to a nearby stream and stand on the middle of the bridge which crosses it.

There we have great fun collecting a little pile of twigs or fallen leaves and tossing them over the side of the bridge, one by one, waiting to see whose will be the first to come through on the other side. Then we stand and watch patiently as the water carries our little "boats" downstream and out of sight.

It is something I like to think about if I have had a day when nothing seems to go right. It's the easiest thing in the world to allow all our irritations and annoyances to linger on, spoiling the rest of the day for us. It is far better, I believe, to let them float away out of sight — just like our boats.

SATURDAY—SEPTEMBER 25.

AS we go about our daily lives, here are two sayings to think about today:

"If God be for us, who can be against us?"

"Lord, help me to find goodness in unexpected places — and kindness in unexpected people."

SUNDAY—SEPTEMBER 26.

BUT the hour cometh, and now is, when the true worshippers shall worship the Father in spirit and in truth: for the Father seeketh such to worship him.

John 4:23

MONDAY—SEPTEMBER 27.

I'VE often heard people say: "I'll be glad when this week's over," or perhaps, "Roll on the holidays!" and other similar remarks. But this is just wishing your life away, and time is so very precious, after all. I think that the older you get, perhaps the more you begin to realise this, and wish instead that time would stand completely still for a while.

Whenever I find I'm wishing time away, I always stop myself and turn my thoughts instead to constructively "looking ahead" — and there's a whole world of difference in that. To look ahead is healthy — it keeps us happy, gives us hope and best of all, stops us from aimlessly wishing our time away.

TUESDAY—SEPTEMBER 28.

WHEN I was young an old minister once said something I have never forgotten. He told me: "Some people don't start to pray till the clouds are black and it starts to rain. I pray hardest when the sun is shining. You see, I don't just say 'Please', I say 'Thank you'."

WEDNESDAY—SEPTEMBER 29.

ON one of my country walks an aeroplane flew very low above me. It gave me a bit of a shock as I hadn't really expected the silence to be so rudely shattered, but, when I had drawn breath, my mind turned to man-made inventions and how some of them can indeed be very noisy! As I continued walking, I began to compare our inventions with the miracles of nature.

I then caught sight of a seed falling from a sycamore tree to the ground. It will take root, I told myself, and in time will make another tree. How can all our modern inventions be compared with this old — yet ever new — miracle?

I'm sure you'll agree with me that it is often the quiet miracles of nature which we can rely on to give us cause to stop and wonder.

THURSDAY—SEPTEMBER 30.

THE Lady of the House returned from an "Old Girls' Reunion" one evening. True, the ex-pupils' appearances had changed as had the colour of their hair, and sometimes there were spectacles where none had been worn before. But twinkling eyes and kind smiles were easily recognisable, as were voices and many a lively sense of humour.

The Lady of the House was in an especially happy mood. "You know, Francis," she said, "I really wondered what we would all be like after so many years, but it's good to realise that although we may change in outward appearance, the things that really matter stay with us always."

October

FRIDAY—OCTOBER 1.

THE Lady of the House was in a philosophical mood one morning.

"Have you ever considered," she mused, "how all the pieces of our lives fit together?" She went on to describe times and places, meetings and partings, and I knew just what she meant.

I reflected for a moment, remembering something that I'd once found on the pages of an old book: "Surely there are in everyone's life certain connections, twists and turns which pass awhile under the category of chance, but at last, well examined, prove to be the very hand of God."

Afterwards, we both felt more content with the great and mysterious jigsaw called life.

SATURDAY—OCTOBER 2.

"NOW, just look at that!" exclaimed Alfred. He was standing in his garden gazing at a tree ablaze with Autumn colours. Red, yellow and orange leaves fluttered in the sunshine.

"If that's what growing old does for you," he beamed, "I'm looking forward to it!"

That's the spirit.

SUNDAY—OCTOBER 3.

AND the grace of our Lord was exceeding abundant with faith and love which is in Christ Jesus.

Timothy 1 1:14

MONDAY—OCTOBER 4.

ONCE a heated discussion was taking place on the bad behaviour of some schoolchildren. The meeting grew noisier and noisier until at last a young woman stood up and said quietly, "It's not criticism they need — it's a good example."

TUESDAY—OCTOBER 5.

"WELL, we can't all be Mrs Beetons, I suppose," said Jane, as she removed a tray of sad-looking cakes from the oven. "But I do try," she added.

Yes, she really does — but no matter how hard, her cakes never look like the glossy illustrations in cookery books, her jam stubbornly refuses to set and her pastry is all too often as tough as leather. Yet her larder is never empty, and neither is her cake tin. Why? Because, as Jane herself says, the world is full of good-hearted, kind and clever people ready to help.

Mind you, it isn't as one-sided as it may sound. Jane is never slow at telling a good story — against herself — and many a downhearted neighbour with a lot on his or her mind is sent on their way uplifted by one of Jane's amusing anecdotes.

WEDNESDAY—OCTOBER 6.

I CAME across these quotes recently and I'd like to share them with you:—

What lies ahead is less important than what lies within.

The world's greatest men have also been the world's greatest dreamers. Never discard your dreams!

Life is a challenge, but you can be what you want to be, with just a little courage!

THURSDAY—OCTOBER 7.

TO my mind there is no more pleasant sound than that of church bells heard across a meadow, or the joyful peals after a wedding echoing through village streets.

William Davies must have found the sound of church bells just as welcome when he was walking to his home in Twyford, Hampshire, one October evening in 1753. He had lost his way in thick fog and, unknown to him, was heading straight for the local chalk pit when the bells of the parish church rang out. Realising he was going in the wrong direction, he stopped just in time, right on the edge of the quarry.

In gratitude for the bells that had kept him from danger, he bequeathed a sum of money to provide an annual meal for the bellringers. To this day the bells are rung every year on 7th October, and afterwards the bellringers always enjoy a fine supper.

FRIDAY—OCTOBER 8.

WHEN I was in Newcastle-on-Tyne I had occasion to visit the Ethel Williams Hall, and heard for the first time about the life and work of this wonderful lady. At the turn of the century, many people had good cause to bless her name.

She was one of the first woman doctors and as such was outcast by many of her medical colleagues — both socially and professionally. But she carried on working, almost exclusively in the poorest slums of Newcastle. She often gave her services free of charge and lived frugally.

Her lifelong companion, Miss M. A. Burnip, said of her friend: "Her religious faith was the dynamic force which governed her whole life."

A remarkable woman who did not count the cost of her unstinting service to others. Truly, one of the unsung heroines.

SATURDAY—OCTOBER 9.

ANTHONY TROLLOPE, the 19th-century novelist, had some wise observations to make about reading:

"The habit of reading is the only enjoyment I know in which there is no alloy. It lasts when all other pleasures fade. It will be there to support you when all other resources are gone. It will be present to you when you grow older."

Reflect on these words today and I'm sure you'll agree that there is a lot of truth in them.

SUNDAY—OCTOBER 10.

ASK, and it shall be given you; seek, and ye shall find.

Matthew 7:7

MONDAY—OCTOBER 11.

THE Rev. Sabine Baring-Gould, author of the famous hymn "Onward Christian Soldiers", was a great encourager. On one occasion he watched a young blacksmith shoeing a horse. He obviously did the job well.

Baring-Gould, who was then Squire and Rector of Lew Trenchard, Devonshire, showed him some sketches of ornamental gates he wanted for his home, and asked if the craftsman would do the job. Although it was a completely new challenge, the blacksmith immediately agreed to take on the work.

He succeeded in making some very fine ornate gates — just the type his customer had asked for. Baring-Gould always believed in encouraging people to take up a challenge and so enrich their lives.

It's something we can all do — allow others to realise the potential they don't know they have.

TUESDAY—OCTOBER 12.

HERE is an 18th-century definition of friendship: "Friendship! Mysterious cement of the soul, sweet'ner of life and solder of society."

How true that is!

AUTUMN GOLD

WEDNESDAY—OCTOBER 13.

HOW often do we hear people complain because they are short of time? For the lonely, time can drag, while for the busy, it flies.

One thing we should never do is to waste it. As Gladys Taber, the American writer, so neatly sums up: "We need time to dream, time to remember and time to reach the infinite. Time to be."

Will we try again, today, to make the most of this very precious gift?

THURSDAY—OCTOBER 14.

AT this time of the year, the things that give me real pleasure are the soft muted colours of a late Autumn day — fading golden leaves, pearly grey mornings, amethyst twilights and wisps of mist across the meadows. After the brilliance of the days of sunshine and the dazzling colours of the flowers of high Summer, they bring a quiet restfulness which is a very welcome contrast. Truly, each season changes and brings its own reward, just as in the changing seasons of our life.

Here is a prayer written by Frank Topping which expresses it well. You may like to make it your own today:

"Lord, let me reflect the colours of your love. Let my life be bright with laughter, my speech be gentle, my thinking warm, my actions kind. May all I experience in the spectrum of my days mellow and blend . . . in peace . . . in love . . . in praise."

THE FRIENDSHIP BOOK

IN 1820 John Harris was born in a cottage near Camborne in Cornwall. The eldest of a large family, he was sent to work in the tin mines when he was barely ten years old. As he toiled long hours in conditions which were not ideal, he composed verses in his head.

When he grew up he became known as the Miner Poet, and after many disappointments his work was published. By the time John Harris died in 1884 he was a much-loved figure, with over a dozen books to his credit. His poems deal with the countryside he loved and the simple experiences of humble folk — for example, these lines which describe the thoughts of a miner:

> *When toiling in the darksome mine*
> *As tired as tired could be,*
> *How has the glad thought cheered my soul,*
> *My children watch for me!*
>
> *And as I op'ed the garden gate,*
> *Which led into the lane,*
> *How danced my heart to see once more*
> *The faces at the pane.*

THE novelist Samuel Butler said that life was like having to play a violin solo in public, learning the instrument as we go along. Needless to say, we all make many mistakes, but isn't it heaven when we hit the right note!

SUNDAY—OCTOBER 17.

OPEN thou mine eyes, that I may behold wondrous things out of thy law.

Psalms 119:18

MONDAY—OCTOBER 18.

IT'S October and, according to the old Roman calendar, it is the eighth month of the year. The Anglo-Saxons called it "Winter fylleth" because it signified the beginning of Winter. I prefer the name the Slavs gave to it — "yellow month" — the countryside is at its loveliest with trees adorned in every shade of gold.

October 18th is St Luke's Day, and around that time it is known as St Luke's Little Summer for the weather then can be particularly mild, and even the butterflies will be tempted into the garden for one last fling.

Then as daylight fades, we may draw the curtains, put more coal on the fire and settle down to enjoy the best of the new season's television programmes, or the hobbies we didn't have time for in the Summer. Yes, there's a lot to be said for the month of October!

TUESDAY—OCTOBER 19.

HERE is a "30-second sermon" from my collection for you to reflect on today:
Happiness is built on simple foundations —
The love of beauty,
A sense of humour,
The gift of good friends.

THE FRIENDSHIP BOOK

WEDNESDAY—OCTOBER 20.

I HEARD a story about an African boy who, many years ago, was out walking beside his mother when a white priest came by. The priest raised his hat as he passed, and the boy was astonished for he had never seen his mother treated with such respect by a white person.

Some time later the boy had to spend months in hospital, and each week he was visited by the same priest. As a result, the boy in time embraced a committed Christian faith. The priest was Trevor Huddleston and the boy was Desmond Tutu, later to become Archbishop of Capetown.

It's a story worth repeating, for it reminds us never to underestimate even a small act of kindness. There's no telling what its impact will be and what it may lead to.

THURSDAY—OCTOBER 21.

GIVE me a star to steer by, Lord,
    A gentle breeze to follow me,
Give me an anchor made of hope,
    To hold me in life's stormy sea.
Give me a cabin built of faith,
    A shelter, wheresoe'er I roam,
Light me a distant beacon, Lord,
    So I may chart my safe way home.
Give me a star to steer by, Lord,
    A flowing and a peaceful tide,
As I'm sailing on life's ocean,
    Be my pilot and my guide.

Iris Hesselden.

THE FRIENDSHIP BOOK

FRIDAY—OCTOBER 22.

SOME points to ponder as you go through life today:

Don't worry if your road is all uphill — the view from the top could be breathtaking.

What seems out of reach is nearer than you think — reach out with hope.

SATURDAY—OCTOBER 23.

SOME years ago, a newspaper printed a verse which I find very helpful and I often like to read it again. I have no idea who wrote it, but gladly pass it on to you:

I may not strive to reach the heights,
My place is lowly and obscure;
But if at night I can recall
One helpful deed, however small;
If some bright word I may have said
A soul has cheered and comforted;
If I have tried, at least, to share
The burdens that my neighbours bear;
Then I may count my day well spent,
And sleep with calm and sweet content.

SUNDAY—OCTOBER 24.

AND the peace of God, which passeth all understanding, shall keep your hearts and minds through Christ Jesus.

Philippians 4:7

THE FRIENDSHIP BOOK

MONDAY—OCTOBER 25.

FOR the first time I have read a story about a potato that preached a sermon. A Salvation Army girl was speaking to a crowd of people on a street corner. Many were hostile and one man even took a potato from a bag and threw it. It struck her but she went on speaking, then picked it up and carried it home.

She later planted it in her garden, and at the Harvest Festival service a fine display of potatoes took pride of place. The following day they were taken to a needy old gentleman. So you will see now how a potato could preach a sermon.

TUESDAY—OCTOBER 26.

WHAT a lovely thing it is —
A heart that's warm and kind.
One filled with compassion
That soothes the troubled mind.
A heart that's all forgiving
And always understands,
One who goes the second mile
And never makes demands.

So many hearts grow cold and hard
From knocks upon life's way,
And many lack compassion
In the world today.
Always trim the lamp of love
And keep the flame alight —
The heart filled with compassion
Is lovely in God's sight.

Kathleen Gillum.

WEDNESDAY—OCTOBER 27.

OUR friend Pat loves going round antique shops. Over the years she has found all sorts of "treasures" and her most recent find was a pair of attractive earrings that were "going for a song".

"I fell in love with them," said Pat, "but I didn't believe they would have any real value until I later discovered they were pure gold."

A lucky find indeed — in a material sense. Yet I am sure we can all think of someone we know who symbolises "pure gold", someone who never fails to bring brightness into our life. Let's be thankful for such folk!

THURSDAY—OCTOBER 28.

SUDDEN cracks and creaks can be alarming during the night. I recall a friend who was kept awake in a hotel by gurgling plumbing.

On bemoaning the fact to her room-mate, she received the reply, "Make friends with it!" She asked what on earth that meant.

"Well, you can't do anything about it, can you?" demanded her friend. "So change your attitude to it. Remember, that pipe has to carry water around, passing it on to other pipes, and because it is doing its job well, it sings as it goes, so it's a friendly pipe."

My friend was so intrigued by this that she began to think "friendly thoughts" towards the pipe and fell asleep. If you take the trouble to find out the whys and wherefores, you could "befriend" a great many situations in life.

FRIDAY—OCTOBER 29.

GIVE as much as you can afford;
If you can't afford much —
Give a smile!

Life is like the weather —
To enjoy the rainbow
We must endure the storm.

SATURDAY—OCTOBER 30.

THE sky was grey, and it was raining steadily. A thoroughly cheerless morning, the sort of morning that makes folk feel equally grey! I decided to catch up on some correspondence.

Almost imperceptibly, I became aware of something different. I looked up from my writing desk and realised that the rain had not only stopped, but that there were patches of blue sky pushing the grey clouds further and further apart. And there was the sun, its beams strengthening every minute as it poured through the patio doors filling the room with bright light and comforting warmth.

Dull days come for us all, but don't despair . . . keep going. Do whatever has to be done, and don't give in — the sun will shine again for you!

SUNDAY—OCTOBER 31.

SOME trust in chariots, and some in horses: but we will remember the Name of the Lord our God.

Psalms 20:7

November

ALBERT SCHWEITZER, one of the most brilliant men of his generation, remained humble to the end. He once said:

"As we acquire more knowledge, things do not become more understandable, but more mysterious."

THE Lady of the House and I had both been feeling under the weather suffering from heavy colds. Nothing serious, you know, but the kind of thing which gets you down, especially at the beginning of Winter. We were feeling a little sorry for ourselves, so the gift which came our way right out of the blue was all the more welcome.

Our friend Avril came to the door with a bunch of golden chrysanthemums, thrust them into my hand with the words, "Just to cheer you up," then hurried away.

Well, she was right — they worked wonders. The vase full of floral beauty seemed to light up the room. Dare I say that we started to improve the very same day? Was it a coincidence?

I wonder . . .

WEDNESDAY—NOVEMBER 3.

PAM is one of these folk who always seems to think happy thoughts and do kind things. Now that she is retired, she has time to do some new thoughtful deeds for friends and family.

Pam also keeps a diary every day, and it always seems to be particularly interesting when she has been away on holiday. "We are apt to forget a good deal when we visit new places and see thrilling things, and a camera doesn't capture it all," she says.

We know that Pam enjoys writing her entries, but what we didn't know until recently is that on Winter afternoons she takes her special holiday diaries to read aloud and share her adventures and memories with partially-sighted friends.

Needless to say, to many people, there's nobody, just nobody, quite like Pam.

THURSDAY—NOVEMBER 4.

ONLY a few words, perhaps, but how they made the sun come out! One particularly grey day, we were leaving the house when a cheerful voice called out, "Hello, I haven't seen you for ages!" We turned to reply, as our neighbour continued, "Well, for three days anyway!"

We all laughed and asked each other how we were, then went our separate ways. Not many words, but what a difference they made on a wet, depressing day.

FRIDAY—NOVEMBER 5.

IT'S Bonfire Night and many families will be letting off fireworks, eating hot dogs, jacket potatoes and slabs of sticky parkin round the fire, while the eyes of the children shine as they hold sparklers. As I'm still young at heart, I'll be joining in the fun and watching the colours of the fire vie with the rockets in the sky.

Many, too, will be glad to take the opportunity to dispose of garden rubbish which has collected, and will give a sigh of satisfaction to see it consumed by the flames. Now, what a good idea it would be to write down anything that has upset or annoyed us in the past day or two and see that go up in smoke on the bonfire. I'm sure we would feel so much better for it!

SATURDAY—NOVEMBER 6.

BEFORE the Battle of Edgehill in 1642 during the English Civil War, Sir Jacob Astley prayed: "Lorde, Thou knowest that I must be very busie this day. If I forget thee, yet do not thou forget me."

A prayer as relevant today as it was in 1642, for isn't it easy to forget the really important things in the daily hustle and bustle?

SUNDAY—NOVEMBER 7.

O GIVE thanks unto the Lord; for he is good: for his mercy endureth for ever.

Psalms 136:1

WHEN DAY
IS DONE

MONDAY—NOVEMBER 8.

OUR young friend, Katie, loves going to parties and is most unhappy if she isn't able to have a new dress for the occasion.

It made me reflect on what other people consider to be life's essentials. For example, the Lady of the House needs to have plants and flowers around her whenever possible.

In the novel "Three Men In A Boat" writer Jerome K. Jerome had this to say: "Let your boat of life be light, packed only with what you need — a homely home and simple pleasures, one or two friends worth the name, someone to love and to love you, a cat, a dog, enough to eat and enough to wear . . ."

Let's be satisfied with the simple things of life!

TUESDAY—NOVEMBER 9.

THIS item is from a church magazine sent to me by a friend in Derbyshire:

"Lord, give us a vision for our country.
May it be a land of justice and peace,
Where people do not take unfair advantage
*   of each other;*
Where all have sufficient, and poverty and evil
Will have no place to fester;
Where seeking to serve others means more
*   than honour and success;*
Where order does not rest on force;
Where faith, hope and love flourish,
And all work for the will of God."

THE FRIENDSHIP BOOK

BEFORE the Lady of the House goes out shopping she writes down a list of everything she needs.

"Otherwise," she says, "I'm bound to come home without some necessary item." She has, however, never written a list like the one a widower found among his late wife's effects. It had been written early in their marriage. It said:

"One of these days I must go shopping. I am completely out of self-respect. I want to change the self-righteousness I picked up the other day for some humility, which they say is less expensive and wears better. I want to look for some tolerance which is being used for wraps this season, and I must try to match some patience that my neighbour wears. It is very becoming on her and I think it might look well on me."

A shopping list we could all do well to purchase from.

*F*RIENDSHIP'S *a flower for all seasons,*
It never will fade away,
Lasting with loyalty growing,
Bringing a joy to each day.
Friendship's a gift to be given,
For then, you'll find — and it's true —
By passing it round, there's a promise
Very soon, it will come back to you!

Elizabeth Gozney.

FRIDAY—NOVEMBER 12.

THIS is the story of a young Scot who went to Canada to seek his fortune. He found work as a farm hand, but soon returned to his native country as he was so homesick.

When he was settled at home again, he decided to say "thank you" to the farmer and his wife in Canada who had employed him and tried so hard to make him feel welcome. He bought them a vase, and in the parcel he included a small envelope containing a handful of wheat.

The farmer sowed the grain and found it exactly right for the conditions in Canada; in fact, it provided a better yield than any he had sown before. Over the years many bushels of this variety were grown, after he passed on the seeds to other farmers in the area.

Who can tell what we can achieve when we give away the little that we have to others?

SATURDAY—NOVEMBER 13.

WHAT can give us warm comfort in times of trouble? Why, friendship, of course — for, as it is said, real friendship does not freeze in Winter.

SUNDAY—NOVEMBER 14.

THIS then is the message which we have heard of him, and declare unto you, that God is light, and in him is no darkness at all.

John 1 1:5

MONDAY—NOVEMBER 15.

VISITORS to St John's Church in Keswick can see the grave of Sir Hugh Walpole, the well-known novelist, yet they may not know about the achievements of the first vicar of this fine church.

The Rev. Frederick W. Myers, who was born in 1811, had a considerable influence in the Keswick area. He founded St John's School and Library, playing an important part in educating his people.

He believed in this maxim: "Not in the things that are done for us, but in the things that are done by us, does our true strength lie."

TUESDAY—NOVEMBER 16.

DO you ever make time to visit a church when you are on holiday? It's something I make a point of doing and seldom come away without finding something new to think about. Here are some lines I read during one such visit:

"There is an old Christian tradition that God sends each person into this world:

With a special message to deliver,
With a special song to sing for others,
With a special act of love to bestow.
No one else can speak that message,
Or sing that song,
Or offer that act of love.

These are entrusted only to that one very special person."

It gave a lift to my spirit that day — as I hope it will to yours now.

WEDNESDAY—NOVEMBER 17.

WHERE have all the "saints" gone? Oh, they're still around and, in fact, I heard of just such a one not long ago. She was working in an inner-city mission, and one afternoon she visited an old lady living in a dingy back room.

"I'm praying the Lord will give me somewhere cleaner and brighter to live," said the old lady.

"Right," said the visitor, "let's get down to it."

"But I can't kneel!" came the reply, thinking the mission visitor meant to pray.

"But I can," came the reply, and within moments she was down on her knees, not praying, but scrubbing the floor and mats.

Yes, saints are practical people, you know, and there are still quite a few about.

THURSDAY—NOVEMBER 18.

"PEOPLE seem to have few manners these days," remarked a woman shopper after someone had pushed in front of her.

"She wouldn't have done that if you had looked as if you were somebody important," her companion replied.

This conversation brought to mind these words of George Bernard Shaw in "Pygmalion":—

"The great secret, Eliza, is not having bad manners or good manners, or any other particular set of manners, but having the same manners for all human souls; in short, behaving as if you were in Heaven where there are no third-class carriages and one soul is as good as another."

THE FRIENDSHIP BOOK

FRIDAY—NOVEMBER 19.

I HEARD this story from a golfer friend who lives in St Andrews. One Saturday he was playing golf with a fellow club member, someone he didn't know, who turned out to be a minister. On the fourth hole of the Eden course, the minister hit his ball away to the right — off the fairway and into the estuary of the River Eden which borders the course there.

The minister walked up the fairway to the place where his ball went out of bounds, jumped down to the beach — fortunately the tide was out — tried to find his ball but couldn't.

Meantime, my friend had found his own ball, with another lying right beside it — which, strangely, turned out to be the minister's! It had ricocheted off a rock and bounced back on to the course.

Just when you think all is lost, a situation can often turn round in your favour. Not surprisingly, the minister had some new material for his sermon next day!

SATURDAY—NOVEMBER 20.

I F only we could all take a hint from a postman's mistake. We have a post-box near our house, and some time ago I found that the postman had placed the "Next Collection" sign upside down. Instead of "MON", it read "NOW"!

Maybe it was a message for me to write to some long-neglected friends sooner rather than later.

SUNDAY—NOVEMBER 21.

WE then that are strong ought to bear the infirmities of the weak, and not to please ourselves.

Romans 15:1

MONDAY—NOVEMBER 22.

THE Lady of the House and I visited an elderly friend in a nursing home. Maisie's eyesight is failing and she walks with a stick.

Not much of a life for her, you might say. Surely she must feel downhearted. Well, we had an entertaining afternoon that day as Maisie told us all about her youth, her brothers and sisters and the adventures that they used to have.

"Maybe life isn't quite the same for me these days," she said, "but I have so many happy memories to keep me company. No one can take them away. I'm very fortunate!"

On the way home, we found ourselves hoping that, one day, we would be able to reflect on our circumstances and say the same.

Always remember the sunshine!

TUESDAY—NOVEMBER 23.

HERE are a couple of optimistic sayings to keep in mind when we are facing life's many challenges:

"Life is a great adventure, so face it with courage — and a cheerful heart."

"Seasons come and seasons go — but love goes on for ever."

WEDNESDAY—NOVEMBER 24.

"**P**EOPLE don't choose cats," remarked our friend, Mary, as she stroked the purring tabby on her lap. "Cats choose people." With that she proceeded to tell us how Tilly had come to share her home.

"She was a poor little stray," said Mary. "She looked dirty and frightened, but she must have known that this is a home that loves cats because one day at feeding time she poked her head round the kitchen door — and decided to stay. Now you can see what a beautiful cat she is with a clean, glossy coat. She's regained her confidence and feels quite at home!"

So the story of one poor, stray cat had a happy ending. It isn't only animals, though, that need our care. There may be a lonely old person just longing to be invited to call in for a cup of tea with the warm and happy family across the road.

Always remember there could be someone waiting for a friendly word or a helping hand.

THURSDAY—NOVEMBER 25.

WE all have dark times in our lives, when we long for a little light to cheer us on our way. Perhaps on such occasions we will find it in these lines by Oliver Goldsmith:

Hope, like the glimmering taper's light,
Adorns and cheers our way,
And still, as darker grows the night,
Emits a brighter ray.

FRIDAY—NOVEMBER 26.

THREE thoughts for you to consider today:

Show a little kindness —
It will return to you
From a different direction.

Climbing the ladder of ambition
Is often difficult. Falling off is very easy.

Love never falters; love never fails —
Love is eternal.

SATURDAY—NOVEMBER 27.

IT was Winter time and snow lay on the ground but the Lady of the House decided, in spite of the cold, to visit our friend Barbara who has a cottage in the Lake District.

After long walks in the bitter wind we returned each evening to a lovely home-cooked meal and a fragrant fire. Barbara was burning pear, apple and cherry logs — the cottage had a delightful aroma of Summer.

Barbara's company and those warm fires revived both mind and body — far better than any medicine from a bottle, surely! Later, I happened to read these words by G. K. Chesterton which were particularly apt: —

"A queer fancy seems to be current that a fire exists only to warm people. It exists also to light their darkness, to raise their spirits . . ."

We will never forget Barbara's beautiful fires — they certainly brought a special warmth to us.

SUNDAY—NOVEMBER 28.

TAKE therefore no thought for the morrow: for the morrow shall take thought for the things of itself.

Matthew 6:34

MONDAY—NOVEMBER 29.

I WAS in Canterbury recently and had an hour to spare, so I went to the cathedral and mingled with the other visitors, admiring the beauty of the building and praying.

I made my way to the grave of the beloved Archbishop William Temple, and remembered a little story that I once read about him. It seems that when he was at school a master had been marking one of his essays.

As he gave it back to William he told him that it was a good try, and then said, "But don't you think you went out of your depth?"

Young William replied, "Maybe, but how else can I learn to swim?"

All through his life William thought like this, never fearing to embrace new ideas, not knowing where they would lead. Let us pray for courage to take more steps in the dark — as he did.

TUESDAY—NOVEMBER 30.

KEEP a twinkle in your eye,
A smile on your lips,
And a friend in your heart.

Anon.

December

"IN the depths of Winter, I finally learned that within me there lay an invincible Summer." So wrote the French philosopher Albert Camus and how wonderful, in the dark days of Winter, to reach down into that inner light.

We all have loving memories, bright and sunny thoughts and many portions of happiness, large and small. Let us keep them safe within us and our "inner Summer" will surely carry us through, until Spring returns once more.

OUR friend, Jenny, took her five-year-old daughter, Katy, to visit great-aunt Nell in a residential home. Katy thoroughly enjoyed carrying round the biscuits at afternoon tea-time, and completely forgot her shyness. So much so, in fact, that when she came to one particularly elderly resident, she asked solemnly:

"Are you very old?" The senior citizen looked down at the anxious little face and smiled.

"No, lass, I wouldn't say I was old, but I must admit I've been young for an awful long time!"

And may she continue to be "young" in the future.

FRIDAY—DECEMBER 3.

MANY readers will remember Gracie Fields with affection, the Lancashire lass who became a worldwide success through her singing and music hall acts.

Once, when speaking of the early years of her career, she pointed out: "It was nothing more than using abilities. One thing that made me happy was a sense of striving, the hope of getting somewhere. It still gives me happiness to have this feeling."

Her philosophy can be adopted by us all. Whether it is writing a short story or perhaps painting a favourite scene — the sense of striving plays an important part.

It enriches our own lives and very often that of others. But if we don't try we never get anywhere, do we?

SATURDAY—DECEMBER 4.

I DO like this description of true friendship by the 17th-century German poet Simon Dahl. I hope you do, too.

"Then come the wild weather, come sleet or snow
We will stand by each other, however it blow."

SUNDAY—DECEMBER 5.

BE ye therefore perfect, even as your Father which is in heaven is perfect.

Matthew 5: 48

THE FRIENDSHIP BOOK

I WAS once in London on holiday. Later, looking back on my stay, I remembered some small acts of kindness I'd noticed.

For example, I'd seen three rather unkempt-looking youths jostling their way along the pavement laughing and joking. They suddenly stopped to help an elderly gentleman across the square — they had come to his aid while others had simply passed by. Then I noticed a businesswoman spending five precious minutes explaining something to a Japanese tourist.

These people may never have a statue erected in their memory, but to me they are important. They will be remembered for their thoughtfulness.

THE Lady of the House and I decided to visit a local craft shop and tea-room. There were many attractive gifts on display, but the things which appealed most were colourful fridge magnets. There were many designs to cheer up the kitchen inscribed with quotations. One of my favourites was: "You've got to believe to achieve."

How true, I thought. We need to have faith in ourselves if we are to accomplish anything. We all need help at some time, whether from our friends and loved ones, or from something deep inside us to carry on and never give up.

Each morning, I look at the motto and it gives me confidence to face the day.

THE FRIENDSHIP BOOK

ONE of the most successful female hymn writers was the American Fanny Crosby, born in 1820, who later wrote her many compositions under her married name of Frances Van Alstyne.

She made a contract with a publisher to produce at least three new hymns a week and her output was to be 8,000 in total — and all in spite of being left blind when she was a mere six weeks old. Sankey and Moody, the famous American evangelists, used Fanny's hymns widely and, much later, in the London Crusade in 1954, Billy Graham made "To God Be The Glory" the theme song.

Fanny also found time to teach, lecture and take a keen interest in local affairs. A most industrious lady! So when you next sing "To God Be The Glory", "Blessed Assurance", "Rescue The Perishing" or "Safe In The Arms Of Jesus", perhaps you will remember that determined and hardworking lady.

HERE are some wise words to bear in mind today:

Yesterday belongs to the past, tomorrow belongs to you — use it wisely.

Dream more than others expect and you will be more than others think is possible.

LAKELAND
LOOKING-GLASS

FRIDAY—DECEMBER 10.

I ENJOYED walking the hills when I was young, and there was nothing more uplifting than to be off with my rucksack, the lark and the curlew my only company. Often I reached home exhausted. Strange, though, how refreshed I always felt the following morning.

One time, a year or two ago, I was invited to spend a few days in the Lake District with an old friend who knew the quiet ways and how to reach many deserted places. It was all so beautiful and the years simply rolled away.

On my return, I felt strengthened and refreshed, just as I used to when I was younger. In the ever-changing world the hills remind us that some things are changeless and eternal. The words of Arthur Guiterman came back to me:

God, give me hills to climb,
And strength for climbing!

SATURDAY—DECEMBER 11.

SOMEONE once told me this: if you see a friend in trouble, don't ask if there is anything you can do. Think of something and do it.

SUNDAY—DECEMBER 12.

I WILL lay me down in peace, and take my rest: for it is thou, Lord, only, that makest me dwell in safety.

Psalm 4:8

MONDAY—DECEMBER 13.

OUR young friend Michelle has just returned from the holiday of a lifetime spent in New York. She was impressed with the generous hospitality of all her new-found friends and we spent a pleasant evening with her, sharing her experiences.

Among her many holiday souvenirs which she proudly showed us, the one which gave the most pleasure was a present from her hostess, following a lovely custom in the Albany region. It was a small silver brooch in the shape of an angel and the card accompanying it said: "I am your guardian angel, given by someone who loves and cares about you."

The custom derives from the belief that every individual has an angel assigned by God as guardian. Perhaps this is how the old rhyme originated, the one many will associate with childhood prayers:

"Matthew, Mark, Luke and John,
Bless the bed that I lie on,
Four angels guard my head . . ."

TUESDAY—DECEMBER 14.

I'D like to share these thoughts with you today from my book of quotations:

"Happiness is frost on the window, and slippers by the fire."

"Be kind to others — be good to yourself now and then."

WEDNESDAY—DECEMBER 15.

IT is quite usual nowadays to see students and lecturers listening intently while older people recall events from their childhood. Many such reminiscences are recorded by oral history units.

One lady, when chided that she had left out the unpleasant recollections, retorted, "By the bad bits, I suppose you mean when my father's wages didn't go far enough and we had no luxuries like holidays abroad? Well, we may not have been rich but we enjoyed many happy times."

It's surely all to do with a more contented attitude.

THURSDAY—DECEMBER 16.

A YOUNG friend of mine was exasperated by something that her brother was telling her. She said, "That comment came out of your mouth without going through your brain first!"

Many people, too, seem to speak with authority on subjects they know little about. They can make us feel that they have a solution to every problem — but life is not like that.

Friends of the late Adlai Stevenson, the American statesman who served his country well at the United Nations, said he had learned that there is a time to speak and a time to stay silent.

So today, let us all try to think before we speak and to remember the little prayer:

God be in my head,
and in my understanding;
God be in my mouth,
and in my speaking.

FRIDAY—DECEMBER 17.

VISITING our friend Mary, I found her cutting snippets out of newspapers and placing them in an empty chocolate box.

She told me that it had been a present, and once the contents had been eaten, she wondered how to put it to good use. Then she read a letter in her local paper bemoaning all the negative news.

That set Mary thinking — and searching. Sure enough, she did find some good news, kindly deeds and heart-warming events. That gave her just the right opportunity to use the box, and into it she now puts the uplifting news reports. They remind her that there is still much in the world to be happy about.

What a worthwhile idea!

SATURDAY—DECEMBER 18.

MANY children might complain if their birthday happens to fall near Christmas. This is what happened to American Annie Ide. Her father was a government official and later Chief Justice of Samoa, the island home of the famous Scottish author, Robert Louis Stevenson. Hearing of her distress at not having a "private" birthday, R.L.S. decided to do something about it.

He drew up a deed transferring his own birthday to Annie. This looked like an official legal document — R.L.S. said that he had attained the age when he had no further use for it.

The manner in which any gift is given adds a certain something to the occasion.

ROCK OF AGES

SUNDAY—DECEMBER 19.

BEHOLD, a virgin shall be with child, and shall bring forth a son, and they shall call his name Emmanuel, which being interpreted is, God with us.

Matthew 1:23

MONDAY—DECEMBER 20.

THE Lady of the House and I were quietly enjoying a cup of tea once after a trip to view the Christmas lights, when she remarked, "Francis, have you ever thought just how much others, often complete strangers, contribute brightness to the special joys of Christmas?

"Just think, if nobody took the trouble to put Christmas trees at their windows and Christmas wreaths on their front doors, where we as passers-by can enjoy them, too, wouldn't we miss them? We'd also miss the lights in our town centres, the carol singers and the decorated shop windows."

How true. Isn't it easy to accept other people's efforts without thinking much about them?

TUESDAY—DECEMBER 21.

A GROUP of children had been rehearsing for the Nativity play they were to perform for parents. All went well on the day, until one of the shepherds decided to use his initiative.

Approaching the manger, he looked at the baby Jesus, smiled at Mary and said, "Isn't he like his dad?"

THE FRIENDSHIP BOOK

TODAY is my favourite day! It is the shortest day of the year — it may well be cold, dark, wet, foggy or blustery, yet that is exactly why it happens to mean so much to me.

From now on, however imperceptibly, the days will begin to lengthen, the birds will eventually break into song again and all around us we shall see the first welcome signs of Spring. Best of all, Christmas is only three days away!

That's why, I repeat, today is my favourite day, and I hope you'll be able to enjoy it, too.

GEORGE HERBERT, a 17th-century country parson, knew that love could be shown by the practical care of those in need.

One day, he set out from his home in the little village of Bemerton to join friends in Salisbury who met regularly to make music. As he was walking along, he saw a poor man whose horse had fallen over because its load had slipped.

The minister immediately stopped to help. It was quite a struggle for both the men and the horse, so when the task was completed George Herbert gave the man money to buy refreshments for himself — and his horse.

At last, he was able to join his friends. They were surprised at his lateness and his dirty clothes. After telling them what had happened, he said: "I pray for all in distress, and so far as it is in my power I must practise what I pray for."

FRIDAY—DECEMBER 24.

LOOKING through a box of books at a church bazaar, I found an old schoolbook. Among the lessons was an anonymous poem entitled "Something Each Day". It touched a chord and so I pass on one of the verses to you today:

Something each day — a word —
We cannot know its power;
It grows in fruitfulness
As grows the gentle flower.
What comfort it may bring
Where all is dark and drear!
For a kind word every day
Makes pleasant all the year.

SATURDAY—DECEMBER 25.

I ALWAYS think of the American writer Washington Irving as a man of reconciliation and peace. His book of essays, "The Sketchbook Of Geoffrey Crayon", was immensely popular.

And it is from one of those essays, "Christmas Day", that I have chosen a festive reading for you. The words are spoken by Geoffrey's host in England, Squire Bracebridge.

"I love," the Squire said, "to see this day well kept by rich and poor; it is a great thing to have one day in the year, at least, when you are sure of being welcome wherever you go, and of having, as it were, the world all thrown open to you . . ."

These are words which capture the true spirit of Christmas, don't you agree? A very happy Christmas to you all!

FREEZE FRAME

SUNDAY—DECEMBER 26.

GLORY to God in the highest, and on earth peace, good will toward men.

Luke 2:14

MONDAY—DECEMBER 27.

HAVE you ever thought how rarely we seem to hear folk whistling nowadays? It was common when I was young, but then people didn't have their own personal stereos and the like.

The thought occurred to me when we had a new milkman. Early in the morning, however dark and cold, we heard Jim whistling as he hurried down the path. When he called back to collect his money, I said, "It's a pleasure to meet someone so cheerful."

He then explained how many of his customers were elderly and living alone. They were often nervous if they heard footsteps, but his whistling seemed to reassure them.

It made me pause and think how often kindness goes completely unnoticed. I had a new respect for Jim, our cheerful and thoughtful whistling milkman.

TUESDAY—DECEMBER 28.

WHAT kind of world do we live in? The answer lies, not out there, but in ourselves. A wise man once remarked that a hostile person lives in a hostile world while a loving person finds it a loving one.

WEDNESDAY—DECEMBER 29.

I HAVE been reading what the famous and the not so famous have to say about time:

"Dost thou love life? Then do not squander time, for it is the stuff life is made of."
(Benjamin Franklin)

"I have so much to do today that I shall spend the first three hours in prayer."
(Martin Luther)

THURSDAY—DECEMBER 30.

HERE are some cheerful words to think about: "Long-ago laughter and far-away times hold a special place in our hearts."

FRIDAY—DECEMBER 31.

ON New Year's Eve in Rome many people keep up the old custom of throwing something old out of the window as a symbolic gesture — out with the old, in with the new is the general idea.

A good idea, although I'm not suggesting we throw old bits of furniture and crockery out of the window! But what about opening a window on New Year's Eve and, so to speak, getting rid of negative thoughts?

What a relief to have our minds free to receive new and positive ideas to usher in the New Year.

The Photographs

SHADY RILL — *Groombridge, East Sussex.*
WINTER'S CLOAK — *Cirencester Park, The Cotswolds.*
LOOKING AND LEARNING — *Colne Valley Museum, Golcar, West Yorkshire.*
MORNING HAS BROKEN — *Queen's View, Loch Tummel, Perthshire.*
FARMYARD FRIENDS — *Hay-on-Wye, Powys.*
NET WORK — *Hastings, East Sussex.*
BIRDS'-EYE VIEW — *Wasdale, Cumbria.*
STILL WATERS — *River Thurne, Norfolk.*
RURAL REFLECTIONS — *Staunton, Gloucestershire.*
REST AND BE THANKFUL — *Brimham Rocks, Yorkshire.*
WHERE THE HEART IS — *Woking, Surrey.*
COASTAL CALM — *St Ives, Cornwall.*
A GUIDING HAND — *Troutbeck, Cumbria.*
WAITING AND HOPING — *Dent, North Yorkshire.*
BLUE HAVEN — *Near Cowes, Isle of Wight.*
NATURE'S GLORY — *Ardencraig Gardens, Rothesay.*
HORSE POWER — *Grand Western Canal, Tiverton, Devon.*
FOLLOWING THE PATH — *Roseberry Topping, North Yorkshire.*
A TOUCH OF TRANQUILLITY — *Lake of Menteith, The Trossachs, Scotland.*
AUTUMN GOLD — *Ullswater, Cumbria.*
WHEN DAY IS DONE — *The Moray Firth, Scotland.*
GONE FISHING — *Linlithgow, Midlothian.*
LAKELAND LOOKING-GLASS — *Rydal Water, Cumbria.*
ROCK OF AGES — *Near Torness, East Lothian.*
FREEZE FRAME — *Glen Etive, Argyll.*

ACKNOWLEDGEMENTS: **Andy Williams;** Shady Rill, Where The Heart Is, Blue Haven, Horse Power. **David Askham;** Best Friends, Finding The Way. **Paul Felix;** Winter's Cloak, Farmyard Friends, Rural Reflections. **Ivan J. Belcher;** Transport Of Delight, Still Waters. **Clifford Robinson;** Looking And Learning, Rest And Be Thankful, Waiting And Hoping, Following The Path. **Iain White;** Morning Has Broken. **V. K. Guy;** Net Work, Birds'-Eye View, Coastal Calm, A Guiding Hand, Autumn Gold, Lakeland Looking-Glass. **Steve Hines;** Home Sweet Home. **Douglas Laidlaw;** Nature's Glory. **Robert Scott Photography;** A Touch Of Tranquillity. **Donald Watt Photography;** Harvest Home. **Dennis Hardley Photography;** When Day Is Done, Gone Fishing, Rock Of Ages, Freeze Frame.

Printed and Published by D. C. Thomson & Co., Ltd.,
185 Fleet Street, London EC4A 2HS.
© D. C. Thomson & Co., Ltd., 1998   **ISBN** 0-85116-671-7